W9-CDZ-536

Read Well Science Digest: Food Chains

Teacher's Guide

Unit 17

-ity

as in acti**vity**

-sion

as in permis**sion**

Note: See New and Important Objectives on page 2 for a complete list of skills taught and reviewed.

Critical Foundations in Primary Reading

Marilyn Sprick, Ann Watanabe, Karen Akiyama-Paik, and Shelley V. Jones

Copyright 2009 Sopris West Educational Services. All rights reserved.

Sopris West®
EDUCATIONAL SERVICES
A Cambium Learning® Company

BOSTON, MA · LONGMONT, CO

ISBN 13-digit: 978-1-60218-540-1
ISBN 10-digit: 1-60218-540-9

13 12 11 10 09 08   1 2 3 4 5 6

167003

Table of Contents
Unit 17
Read Well Science Digest: Food Chains

How to Teach the Lessons

End of the Unit

Letter Sounds and Combinations

Cumulative Review of *Read Well 1* Sounds and Combinations (Ss, Ee, ee, Mm, Aa, Dd, th, Nn, Tt, Ww, Ii, Th, Hh, Cc, Rr, ea, sh, Sh, Kk, -ck, oo, ar, wh, Wh, ě, -y as in fly, Ll, Oo, Bb, all, Gg, Ff, Uu, er, oo as in book, Yy, a schwa, Pp, ay, Vv, Qq, Jj, Xx, or, Zz, a_e, -y as in baby, i_e, ou, ow as in cow, ch, Ch, ai, igh, o_e, ir) and:

Unit 2		Unit 3		Unit 5	Unit 6
aw	ew	ue	u_e	ow	ge
/aw/	/o͞o/	/o͞o/	/o͞o/	/ō͞ō/	/j/
Paw	**Crew**	**Blue**	**Flute**	**Snow**	**Page**
Voiced	Voiced	Voiced	Bossy E Voiced	Voiced (Long)	Voiced

Unit 6	Unit 7		Unit 8		Unit 10
-dge	ci	ce	kn	ph	oa
/j/	/sss/	/sss/	/nnn/	/fff/	/ō͞ō/
Badge	**Circle**	**Center**	**Knee**	**Phone**	**Boat**
Voiced	Unvoiced	Unvoiced	Voiced	Unvoiced	Voiced (Long)

Unit 11		Unit 12		Unit 13
oi	ea	gi	au	oy
/oi/	/ěěě/	/j/	/au/	/oy/
Point	**Bread**	**Giraffe**	**Astronaut**	**Boy**
Voiced	Voiced (Short)	Voiced	Voiced	Voiced

Affixes (including morphographs—affixes taught with meaning) and Open Syllables

Cumulative Review of *Read Well 1* Affixes (-ed, -en, -es, -ing, -ly, -s, -y, -tion) and:

Unit 2	Unit 3		Unit 5		Unit 6
re-	un-	ex-	o	-ful	bi-
Means again	**Means not**		Open syllable /ō/	**Means full of**	**Means two**
as in reread	as in unhappy	as in excited	as in open and moment	as in colorful	as in bicycle

Unit 7	Unit 8	Unit 11	Unit 12	Unit 13	
de-	-able	i	be-	-ous	dis-
as in detective	as in comfortable	Open syllable /ī/ as in silence and pilot	as in before	as in enormous	as in discover

Unit 14		Unit 15		Unit 16	
-al	-ible	-or	-ment	-ic	pre-
		Means one who			**Means before**
as in animal	as in flexible	as in actor	as in apartment	as in scientific	as in preview

Unit 17		Unit 18		Unit 19	
-ity	-sion	-ness	-less	in-	im-
			Means without		**Means not**
as in activity	as in permission	as in fairness	as in helpless	as in insert	as in impossible

Introduction
Read Well Science Digest: Food Chains

Sun · Grass · Deer · Cougar

Story Notes

Explore the complex world of food chains with our magazine of science and literature for kids.

Science: Through photography and text, students learn the basics of food chains as they trace the transfer of energy from the sun to green plants, then to herbivores and carnivores.

The *Science Digest* is full of questions. What animal is black and white, smiles, and makes whuffling sounds? A panda? A skunk? A killer whale? What carnivore is at the top of the chain? You might be surprised to find that one lazy predator sleeps 21 hours a day.

Finally, through humor and letters to the editor, enjoy learning about the important role of the great decomposer—the not-so-yucky earthworm.

Literature: Three theme-related poems provide rhythmic interludes to the expository text, and a fictional story brings the recurring theme of community to this food chain unit.

Recommended Read Alouds

The *Read Well 2* suggested Read Alouds enhance small group instruction—providing opportunities to further build background knowledge and vocabulary.

Who Eats What? Food Chains and Food Webs
by Patricia Lauber

Nonfiction • Expository

All living things depend on other living things for survival, and food chains illustrate these connections.

Read Well Connections
Students learn about additional food chains in the suggested Read Aloud. Encourage them to find similarities between these and the ones they read about in the *Read Well Science Digest*.

> **CAUTION**
> **(Reminder)**
> Do not read the Read Aloud recommendations during small group instruction. Reserve this time for students to read.

NOTE FROM THE AUTHORS

A FAVORITE

We are excited to introduce the first volume of the *Read Well Science Digest*. The magazine format allowed us to explore the fascinating theme of food chains through expository text, photography, puzzles, poetry, fiction, and letters to the editor. The rapid change of pace across text selections, art, and photography made this unit a favorite among our field test kids. We hope the *Read Well Science Digest* inspires your students to explore the many children's magazines available to young readers.

New and Important Objectives
A Research-Based Reading Program

Phonemic Awareness
Phonics
Fluency
Vocabulary
Comprehension

Phonological and Phonemic Awareness

Blending; Rhyming; Onset and Rime; Counting Syllables

Phonics

Cumulative Letter Sounds and Combinations

Review • Ss, Ee, ee, Mm, Aa, Dd, th, Nn, Tt, Ww, Ii, Th, Hh, Cc, Rr, ea, sh, Sh, Kk, -ck, oo, ar, wh, Wh, ĕ, -y (as in fly), Ll, Oo, Bb, all, Gg, Ff, Uu, er, oo (as in book), Yy, a (schwa), Pp, ay, Vv, Qq, Jj, Xx, or, Zz, a_e, -y (as in baby), i_e, ou, ow (as in cow), ch, Ch, ai, igh, o_e, ir, aw, ew, ue, u_e, ow (as in snow), ge, -dge, ci, ce, kn, ph, oa, oi, ea (as in bread), gi, au, oy

Cumulative Affixes, Morphographs, and Open Syllables

Review • -ed, -en, -er, -es, -est, -ing, -ly, -s, -y, -tion, re-, un-, ex-, o as in open, -ful, bi-, de-, -able, i as in silence, be-, -ous, dis-, -al, -ible, -or, -ment, -ic, pre-

★ New Letter Sounds, Combinations, Affixes, and Morphographs

-ity (as in activity) • activity
-sion (as in permission) • discussion, mission

★ New Proper Nouns

Albany, Austin, Billy, Cara, Mrs. Chen, Dylan, Josephine, Josephine's, Mama's, Michael, Nate, Mr. Phillips, Professor Worm, Science Digest, Ty

★ New Pattern Words

bait, bray, broom, cells, chased, cub, cub's, cubs, curled, drain, ewww, floss, guest, huffs, joking, krill, link, links, lung, lungs, naps, peas, planned, pounce, pride, prides, pump, raked, rakes, roast, rot, rotted, scraps, sells, shaved, shred, sling, slink, slugs, snarls, snoozed, sprout, sprouting, squirm, squirming, stalk, stalks, striped, stripes, tended, thrive, thrives, thriving, waste, weak

---

∗ **Known Pattern Words With Affixes**, **Known Tricky Words With Affixes**, and **Known Multisyllabic Words With Affixes** have base words students have previously read. The words are new in this unit because they have not been previously read with the affix.

★ = New in this unit

Phonics (continued)

*Known Pattern Words With Affixes • airy, bags, beasts, biting, bolder, chains, colds, eaters, fishing, grazers, grazes, hisses, kicking, killer, kills, knocked, knocking, mailed, reuse, ringing, roars, rows, snoozed, snorting, weeding

☆ New Compound and Hyphenated Words

doorbells, earthworm, earthworms, eyesight, flowerpots, grasslands, ladybugs, lookout, meantime, meatballs, midsize, oatmeal, rainwater, sunflower

☆ Other New Multisyllabic Words

annelids, articles, bottles, cabbage, connect, connected, connects, corrected, crawlies, crawly, creepies, decay, decaying, decomposer, defend, digests, editor, energize, energizing, exceptionally, gobble, gobbled, handles, harvest, harvested, impalas, intelligent, lettuce, lioness, lionesses, meadow, meows, muscular, nectar, nibble, nibbled, nomadic, noodle, picnic, recognize, secret, section, seedling, seedlings, sincere, sincerely, single, sleepers, spelling, stuffy, swallowed, swimmers, talent, whinnies, whinny, whuffle, whuffling

*Known Multisyllabic Words With Affixes • antelopes, bellies, crocodiles, enjoyed, giraffes, lions, mistakes, patterns, robins, scurried, simpler, slimies, tunneling

☆ New Tricky Words

aphid, aphids, billions, camouflaged, educate, educated, haiku, health, healthier, healthy, hyenas, nutrients, recycle, ruin, salads, taco, trillions, truth, unique, vacant

*Known Tricky Words With Affixes • friend's, hearts, pulling, shrieked, waters, worm's, wormy, wrestling, zebra's, zebras, zebras'

Fluency

Accuracy, Expression, Phrasing, Rate

Vocabulary

New • connect, decay, decomposer, digest, energy, floss, food chain, link, nomadic, recycle, scurry, thrive, thriving, unique, vacant

Review • carnivore, communicate, community, herbivore, mammal, predator, prey, protect, scarce, survive

Reviewed in Context • amazing, carnivore, community, crouch, dinosaur, herbivore, impressed, local, mammal, neighborhood, perfect, permission, protection, scrumptious, splendid, surface, vibration

Idioms and Expressions

New • educated guess

Comprehension

Unit Genres

Letter from the Editor
Nonfiction • Expository
Poetry • Free Verse
Nonfiction • Humor
Letters to the Editor
Poetry • Haiku
Fiction • Realistic Narrative
Poetry • Rhyming

Comprehension Processes

Build Knowledge: Factual, Procedural, Conceptual

Day	1	2	3	4	5	6
Remember						
Defining	S	S		S		
Identifying (recalling)	S,C	S,C	S,C	S	S,C	C
Using	S	S	S	S	S	
Understand						
Defining (in your own words)	S,C	S	S,C	S		
Describing	S,C	S	S	S	S	
Explaining (rephrasing)	S	S	S	S	S,C	
Illustrating	C				C	
Sequencing	C				C	
Summarizing	S	S,C	S		C	C
Using	S,C	S,C	S	S	S,C	C
Visualizing					C	
Apply						
Demonstrating	S			S		
Explaining (unstated)	S	S	S	S	S	
Illustrating			C			
Inferring	S	S	S,C		S	
Making Connections (relating)	S		S			C
Predicting		S		S	S	
Using	S,C	S,C	S,C	S,C		
Analyze						
Classifying	S	S				
Comparing/Contrasting				S		
Distinguishing Cause/Effect						
Drawing Conclusions			C			
Inferring						
Evaluate						
Making Judgments		S	S		S	
Responding (personal)		S		S	S,C	
Create						
Generating Ideas				C	S	

E = Exercise, S = Storybook, C = Comprehension & Skill

Comprehension (continued)

Skills and Strategies

Day	1	2	3	4	5	6
Priming Background Knowledge	S			S		
Setting a Purpose for Reading		S	S	S	S	
Answering Questions	S	S	S,C	S	S	S
Asking Questions				C		
Visualizing					C	
Comprehension Monitoring/Fix Ups						
Does it Make Sense?	C		C		C	C
Looking Back						
Restating						
Summarizing						
Main Idea		C	E			
Retelling					C	
Supporting Details		C				C
Understanding Text Structure						
Title, Author, Illustrator	S	S	S	S		
Fact or Fiction						
Genre (Classifying)						
Narrative						
Setting					S,C	
Main Character/Traits (Characterization)*				S	S,C	
Goal				S	S,C	
Problem/Solution				S	S,C	
Action/Events/Sequence					S,C	
Outcome/Conclusion					C	
Lesson/Author's Message						
Expository						
Subject/Topic		C	S,C			
Heading						
Supporting Details (Facts/Information)	C	S,C	S,C	S		C
Main Idea		C	E,S,C			C
Using Graphic Organizers						
Chart		C				
Diagram (labeling)	S,C	S				
Hierarchy (topic/detail)		C	C			C
K-W-L						
Map (locating, labeling)						
Matrix (compare/contrast)						
Sequence (linear, cycle, cause and effect)	S,C	S			C	
Story Map					C	
Web						

E = Exercise, S = Storybook, C = Comprehension & Skill

* Narrator

Comprehension *(continued)*

Study Skills

Day	1	2	3	4	5	6
Alphabetical Order			C			
Following Directions						
Locating Information	C	C	C			
Note Taking						
Previewing						
Reviewing		S	S	S	S	
Test Taking	C	C				C
Using Glossary		S		S		
Using Table of Contents	S					
Viewing	S	S	S			
Verifying						

Writing in Response to Reading

Day	1	2	3	4	5	6
Sentence Completion	C	C	C	C	C	
Making Lists						
Sentence Writing			C	C	C	
Story Retell/Summary					C	
Fact Summary		C				
Paragraph Writing		C		C	C	C
Report Writing						
Open-Ended Response						
Creative Writing						

Writing Traits

(Addressed within the context of Writing in Response to Reading)

Day	1	2	3	4	5	6
Ideas and Content						
Elaborating/Generating		C		C		
Organization						
Introduction						
Topic Sentence		C				C
Supporting Details		C				C
Sequencing					C	
Word Choice						
Sophisticated Words (Tier 2 and 3)		C				
Conventions						
Capital		C	C	C	C	C
Ending Punctuation	C	C	C	C	C	C
Other (commas, quotation marks)				C		
Presentation						
Handwriting		C		C	C	C
Neatness		C		C	C	C

E = Exercise, S = Storybook, C = Comprehension & Skill

Daily Lesson Planning

Teacher-Directed 45 Minutes		Independent Teacher-Directed, as needed
Lesson Part 1 (Phonological Awareness, Phonics, Fluency, Comprehension) 15–20 Minutes	**Lesson Part 2** (Vocabulary, Fluency, Comprehension) 20–25 Minutes	**Lesson Part 3** (Vocabulary, Fluency, Comprehension) 15–20 Minutes
• Exercises	• Unit and/or Story Opener • Vocabulary • Interactive Story Reading • Short Passage Practice Timed Readings	• Story Reading With Partner or Whisper Reading • Comprehension and Skill Activities

HOMEWORK

Read Well 2 Homework (blackline masters of new *Read Well 2* passages) provides an opportunity for children to celebrate accomplishments with parents. Homework should be sent home on routine days.

ORAL READING FLUENCY ASSESSMENT

Upon completion of this unit, assess each student and proceed to Unit 18, as appropriate.

WRITTEN ASSESSMENT

During the time students would normally complete Comprehension and Skill Activities, students will be administered a Written Assessment that can be found on page 115 in the student's *Activity Book 3*.

Note: See Making Decisions for additional assessment information.

DIFFERENTIATED LESSON PLANS

The differentiated lesson plans illustrate how to use materials for students with various learning needs. As you set up your unit plan, always include *Read Well 2* Exercises and Story Reading on a daily basis. Unit 17 includes 6-, 8-, 9-, 10-, and 11-Day Plans.

Plans	For groups that:
6-DAY	Complete Oral Reading Fluency Assessments with Passes and Strong Passes
8-DAY	Complete Oral Reading Fluency Assessments with Passes and require teacher-guided assistance with Story Reading and Comprehension and Skill Work
9-, 10-, or 11-DAY	Have difficulty passing the unit Oral Reading Fluency Assessments

6-DAY PLAN

Day 1	Day 2	Day 3
Teacher-Directed	**Teacher-Directed**	**Teacher-Directed**
• Exercise 1	• Exercise 2	• Exercise 3a
• Unit Opener: Read Well Science Digest: Food Chains	• Vocabulary Power! 2	• Exercise 3b: Focus Lesson
• Letter From the Editor	• What's Black and White and Loved by All?	• Vocabulary Power! 3
• Vocabulary Power! 1	• Guide practice, as needed, on Comp & Skill 3, 4	• 10 Great Reasons to Be an Earthworm
• Links in the Chain, A Food Chain Puzzle, Drain Your Brain About the Chain	**Independent Work**	• Guide practice, as needed, on Comp & Skill 5, 6
• Guide practice, as needed, on Comp & Skill 1, 2	• On Your Own: Partner or Whisper Read, What's at the Top?, Predators	**Independent Work**
Independent Work	• Comp & Skill 3, 4	• On Your Own: Partner or Whisper Read, More About the 10 Great Reasons to Be an Earthworm
• On Your Own: Partner or Whisper Read, From Grass to Meatballs	**Homework**	• Comp & Skill 5, 6
• Comp & Skill 1, 2	• Homework Passage 2	**Homework**
Homework		• Homework Passage 3
• Homework Passage 1		

Day 4	Day 5	Day 6
Teacher-Directed	**Teacher-Directed**	**Teacher-Directed**
• Exercise 4	• Exercise 5	• Exercise 6
• Vocabulary Power! 4	• The Garden We Share, Ch. 2	• Fluency, Links in a Food Chain
• Digging Up the Truth, Garden Haiku	• Guide practice, as needed, on Comp & Skill 9, 10a, 10b	**Independent Work**
• Guide practice, as needed, on Comp & Skill 7, 8	**Independent Work**	• Repeated Reading: Partner or Whisper Read, Links in a Food Chain
Independent Work	• On Your Own: Partner or Whisper Read, The Garden We Share, Ch. 3	• Written Assessment
• On Your Own: Partner or Whisper Read, The Garden We Share, Ch. 1	• Comp & Skill 9, 10a, 10b	• Oral Reading Fluency Assessment*
• Comp & Skill 7, 8	**Homework**	**Homework**
Homework	• Homework Passage 5	• Homework Passage 6
• Homework Passage 4		

Note: Unit 17 features a Just for Fun Comp & Skill activity, located after Activity 8. This page can be used any time after Exercise 4 and Chapter 1 of "The Garden We Share." The Just for Fun activity allows the related activities, story map and written retell, to be located side by side in the Activity Book.

* The Oral Reading Fluency Assessments are individually administered by the teacher while students are working on their Written Assessments.

Day 1

Teacher-Directed
- Exercise 1
- Unit Opener
- Letter From the Editor
- Vocabulary Power! 1
- Links in the Chain, A Food Chain Puzzle, Drain Your Brain About the Chain
- Guide practice, as needed, on Comp & Skill 1, 2

Independent Work
- On Your Own: Partner or Whisper Read, From Grass to Meatballs
- Comp & Skill 1, 2

Homework
- Homework Passage 1

Day 2

Teacher-Directed
- Exercise 2
- Vocabulary Power! 2
- What's Black and White and Loved by All?
- Guide practice, as needed, on Comp & Skill 3

Independent Work
- Repeated Reading: Partner or Whisper Read, What's Black and White and Loved by All?
- Comp & Skill 3

Homework
- Homework Passage 2

Day 3

Teacher-Directed
- Review Exercise 1
- What's At the Top?, Predators
- Guide practice, as needed, on Comp & Skill 4

Independent Work
- Repeated Reading: Partner or Whisper Read, What's At the Top?, Predators
- Comp & Skill 4

Homework
- Extra Practice Word Fluency A

Day 4

Teacher-Directed
- Exercise 3a
- Exercise 3b: Focus Lesson
- Vocabulary Power! 3
- 10 Great Reasons to Be an Earthworm
- Guide practice, as needed, on Comp & Skill 5, 6

Independent Work
- On Your Own: Partner or Whisper Read, More About the 10 Great Reasons to Be an Earthworm
- Comp & Skill 5, 6

Homework
- Homework Passage 3

Day 5

Teacher-Directed
- Exercise 4
- Vocabulary Power! 4
- Digging Up the Truth, Garden Haiku
- Guide practice, as needed, on Comp & Skill 7, 8

Independent Work
- On Your Own: Partner or Whisper Read, The Garden We Share, Ch. 1
- Comp & Skill 7, 8

Homework
- Homework Passage 4

Day 6

Teacher-Directed
- Exercise 5
- The Garden We Share, Ch. 2
- Guide practice, as needed, on Comp & Skill 9, 10a, 10b

Independent Work
- On Your Own: Partner or Whisper Read, The Garden We Share, Ch. 3
- Comp & Skill 9, Begin 10a, 10b

Homework
- Homework Passage 5

Day 7

Teacher-Directed
- Review Exercise 3a
- Review Think and Talk, p. 58
- Reread, The Garden We Share, Ch. 3
- Assist with Comp & Skill 10a, 10b, as needed

Independent Work
- Repeated Reading: Student or Teacher's Choice
- Complete Comp & Skill 10a, 10b

Homework
- Comp & Skill 8 (Passage Fluency)

Day 8

Teacher-Directed
- Exercise 6
- Fluency, Links in a Food Chain

Independent Work
- Repeated Reading: Partner or Whisper Read, Links in a Food Chain
- Written Assessment
- Oral Reading Fluency Assessment*

Homework
- Homework Passage 6

Day 9 Extra Practice 1

Teacher-Directed
- Decoding Practice
- Fluency Passage

Independent Work
- Activity and Word Fluency A

Homework
- Fluency Passage

Day 10 Extra Practice 2

Teacher-Directed
- Decoding Practice
- Fluency Passage

Independent Work
- Activity and Word Fluency B

Homework
- Fluency Passage

Day 11 Extra Practice 3

Teacher-Directed
- Decoding Practice
- Fluency Passage

Independent Work
- Activity and Word Fluency A or B
- Oral Reading Fluency Assessment*

Homework
- Fluency Passage

Materials and Materials Preparation

Core Lessons

Teacher Materials

READ WELL 2 MATERIALS

- Unit 17 Teacher's Guide
- Sound Cards
- Unit 17 Oral Reading Fluency Assessment found on page 121
- Group Assessment Record found in the *Assessment Manual*

SCHOOL SUPPLIES

Stopwatch or watch with a second hand

Student Materials

READ WELL 2 MATERIALS (for each student)

- *Read Well Science Digest: Food Chains*
- *Exercise Book 3*
- *Activity Book 3* or copies of Unit 17 Comprehension and Skill Work
- Unit 17 Written Assessment found in *Activity Book 3,* page 115, and on the CD
- Unit 17 Certificate of Achievement/Goal Setting (BLM, pages 122 and 123)
- Unit 17 Homework (blackline masters)
  See *Getting Started* for suggested homework routines.

> Make one copy per student of each blackline master, as appropriate for the group.
>
> *Note:* For new or difficult Comprehension and Skill Activities, make overhead transparencies from the blackline masters. Use the transparencies to demonstrate and guide practice.

SCHOOL SUPPLIES

Pencils, colors (optional—markers, crayons, or colored pencils)

> **FOCUS LESSONS**
>
> For Exercise 3b (Focus Lesson), make an overhead transparency from the blackline masters, write on a transparency placed over the pages, or use paper copies to demonstrate how to complete the lessons.

Extra Practice Lessons

> **CAUTION**
> Use these lessons only if needed. Students who need Extra Practice may benefit from one, two, or three lessons.

Student Materials

READ WELL 2 MATERIALS (for each student, as needed)

See Extra Practice blackline masters located on the CD.

- Unit 17 Extra Practice 1: Decoding Practice, Fluency Passage, Word Fluency A, and Activity
- Unit 17 Extra Practice 2: Decoding Practice, Fluency Passage, Word Fluency B, and Activity
- Unit 17 Extra Practice 3: Decoding Practice, Fluency Passage, Word Fluency A or B, and Activity

SCHOOL SUPPLIES

Pencils, colors (markers, crayons, or colored pencils), highlighters

Important Tips

★Robust Vocabulary Instruction Keeping Words Alive

Research Snapshot

The key to a successful vocabulary program is to use both formal and informal encounters so that attention to vocabulary is happening any time and all the time.

"First, there are vocabulary words taught in conjunction with formal lessons. Second, opportunities arise within the classroom routine that can be used for vocabulary learning . . . Within this verbal environment abundant opportunities exist for drawing attention to vocabulary" (McKeown & Beck, p. 21, 2004).

Read Well 2 provides formal lessons on vocabulary. Words are explicitly taught and introduced before Story Reading. Words are used during reading in stories and in discussions. Then they are often reviewed in Comprehension and Skill activities. Initial word knowledge is built in multiple and purposeful ways in each unit of instruction. Then depth of knowledge is built across units as sophisticated words are used again and again.

You can increase your students' command of the language by encouraging them to use vocabulary words from *Read Well 2* throughout the day. Here are some suggestions for keeping words alive in your classroom.

Thumbs Up: When a student spontaneously uses a new vocabulary word, give the student a thumbs up. Say something like:

[Jaelynn] just used our new vocabulary word *unique*. She said, "Our assembly was unique." Everyone, give [Jaelynn] a thumbs up. What was unique about our assembly?

Vocabulary Stars: Keep a running list of vocabulary words on a bulletin board or chart. When you hear a student use a word, put his or her name and a star next to the word.

Rotate words from previous units in and out of practice.

Vocabulary Stars

exaggerate ★Ryan ★Megan

imaginative ★Dylan ★Ty

exhausted ★Matt ★Jessica

impossible ★Jason ★Jes ★Jen

ordinary ★Josh ★Jaelynn

challenge ★Megan

commotion ★Matt

Content Word Wall: Maintain a content word wall. Start with words from the storybook, then add to the list as students learn additional words related to the theme or topic.

Students may wish to enhance the word wall by illustrating words with magazine pictures and drawings.

Note: Read Well themes and topics are often related to classroom science and social studies instruction.

When *Read Well* instruction precedes related classroom instruction, the *Read Well* unit provides pre-teaching of vocabulary, inspires interest in a topic, and builds prior knowledge.

If science or social studies instruction follows a related *Read Well* unit, the *Read Well* unit provides review of vocabulary and content knowledge and may also extend content knowledge.

Idioms and Expressions: Keep a running list of idioms and expressions. Tally classroom use—yours and students'. Encourage students to add idioms and expressions they hear or use. Use a different color for student-generated idioms and expressions.

If a student uses an idiom or expression, say something like: [Mason], you just used an idiom. *Beats me* is an idiom that means you don't know. Let's put *beats me* on our idiom chart. If you don't know something, you could shrug your shoulders and say . . . beats me.

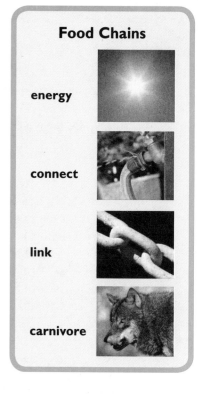

Food Chains

energy

connect

link

carnivore

Idioms and Expressions

bird's-eye view   ⅢⅡ

put your foot down   ⅢⅡ Ⅲ

save the day   ⅢⅠ

caught my eye   ⅢⅡ ⅢⅠ

chain of events   ⅢⅡ

beats me (not in vocab)

Your conscious attention to vocabulary can bring words to life!

How to Teach the Lessons

Teach from this section. Each instructional component is outlined in an easy-to-teach format.

Exercise 1

- Unit Opener, Read Well Science Digest: Food Chains
- Letter from the Editor
- Vocabulary Power! 1
- Story Reading 1
  With the Teacher: Links in the Chain, A Food Chain Puzzle, Drain Your Brain About the Chain
  On Your Own: From Grass to Meatballs
- Comprehension and Skill Activities 1, 2

Exercise 2

- Vocabulary Power! 2
- Story Reading 2
  With the Teacher: What's Black and White and Loved by All?
  On Your Own: What's at the Top?, Predators
- Comprehension and Skill Activities 3, 4

Exercise 3a

- Exercise 3b: Focus Lesson
- Vocabulary Power! 3
- Story Reading 3
  With the Teacher: 10 Great Reasons to Be an Earthworm
  On Your Own: More About the 10 Great Reasons . . .
- Comprehension and Skill Activities 5, 6

Exercise 4

- Vocabulary Power! 4
- Story Reading 4
  With the Teacher: Digging Up the Truth, Garden Haiku
  On Your Own: The Garden We Share, Chapter 1
- Comprehension and Skill Activities 7, 8

Exercise 5

- Story Reading 5
  With the Teacher: The Garden We Share, Chapter 2
  On Your Own: The Garden We Share, Chapter 3
- Comprehension and Skill Activities 9, 10a, 10b

Exercise 6

- Story Reading 6, Fluency
  With the Teacher: Links in a Food Chain
- Written Assessment

Note: Lessons include daily homework.

① SOUND REVIEW

Use selected Sound Cards from Units 1–16.

② SHIFTY WORDS

For each word, have students say the underlined sound. Then have them sound out the word smoothly and say it.

Use the words in sentences, as appropriate.

③ ACCURACY AND FLUENCY BUILDING

- For each task, have students say any underlined part, then read the word.
- Set a pace. Then have students read the whole words in each task and column.
- Provide repeated practice, building accuracy first, then fluency.

C1. Rhyming Words

Have students read each set of rhyming words and identify what's the same about them.

D1. Word Endings

Have students read any underlined word, then the word with an ending.

Note: Tell students that the <u>f</u> in "wolf" and "leaf" changes to a <u>v</u> and that you add <u>e-s</u> to make them plural.

E1. Tricky Words

- For each Tricky Word, have students use the sounds and word parts they know to silently sound out the word. Use the word in a sentence to help with pronunciation.

ocean	Another word for *sea* is . . . *ocean.*
field	A baseball game was being played at the ball . . . *field.*
cougar	A mountain lion is also known as a . . . *cougar.*
butcher	Someone whose job is carving meat is called a . . . *butcher.*
issue	The magazine is printed weekly, and we just got the latest . . . *issue.*
salmon	Dad went fishing and caught a . . . *salmon.*

- Have students go back and read the whole words in the column.

④ WORDS IN CONTEXT

For each word, have students use the sounds and word parts they know to silently sound out the word. Then have students read the sentence. Assist, as needed.

⑤ GENERALIZATION: READING NEW WORDS IN PARAGRAPHS

- Have students read the paragraph silently, then out loud. Tell students to use the sounds and word parts they know to read any difficult words.
- Repeat practice, as needed.

The PACING box (top right):

PACING

Exercise 1 should take about 10 minutes to accommodate the Story Opener.

Science Digest

Unit 17 Exercise 1
Use before Links in the Chain and From Grass to Meatballs

1. **SOUND REVIEW** Use selected Sound Cards from Units 1–16.

2. **SHIFTY WORD BLENDING** For each word, have students say the underlined part, sound out smoothly, then read the word.

t<u>or</u>n	t<u>ow</u>n	<u>br</u>own	br<u>ai</u>n	<u>dr</u>ain

3. **ACCURACY/FLUENCY BUILDING** For each column, have students say any underlined part, then read each word. Next, have them read the column.

A1 Mixed Practice	**B1** Reading by Analogy	**C1** Rhyming Words	**D1** Word Endings	**E1** Tricky Words
r<u>oa</u>st	bl<u>ank</u>	mi<u>llions</u>	<u>eaters</u>	ocean
j<u>oi</u>n	dr<u>ank</u>	bi<u>llions</u>	<u>simpler</u>	field
l<u>i</u>nk	pl<u>ank</u>ton	tri<u>llions</u>		cougar
gr<u>ay</u>			wolf	butcher
s<u>ea</u>l	h<u>ea</u>d	r<u>ai</u>n	wolves	issue
gr<u>a</u>zes	m<u>ea</u>dow	br<u>ai</u>n		salmon
enj<u>oy</u>		ch<u>ai</u>n	leaf	
st<u>ar</u>ve		dr<u>ai</u>n	leaves	

4. **WORDS IN CONTEXT** Have students use the sounds and word parts they know to figure out the word. Then have them read the sentence.

A	en·er·gy	I was so tired after soccer practice, I did not have any <u>energy</u>.
B	ed·i·tor	The spelling mistakes were corrected by the <u>editor</u>.
C	pro·fes·sor	Rick went to school for many years to become a <u>professor</u>.
D	di·gest	Tom enjoyed reading the articles in the Science <u>Digest</u>.
E	con·nect·ed	Your ears are <u>connected</u> to your head.

5. **GENERALIZATION:** Have students read the paragraph silently, then out loud. (New words: guest, salad, tacos)

    Everyone brought food for the neighborhood party. Miss Tam brought red beans and rice. Her guest, Aunty Lani, brought noodle salad. Maya brought tacos, and Ana brought meatballs. There were all kinds of fancy foods. It was a scrumptious meal.

TEAM EXPECTATIONS
(Reminder)

Provide a quick review of expectations before starting the lesson.

1. Sit up.
2. Follow directions.
3. Help each other.
4. Work hard and have fun.

JAZZY PRACTICE

For variety, practice underlined sounds in a jazzy rhythm. Say something like:

Listen to me read Column A1 in a rhythm. I'm going to quickly say each underlined sound two times and then read the word.
/ō/, /ō/, roast;
/oi/, /oi/, join;
/ĭ/, /ĭ/, link.

Your turn. Start at the top of Column A1 and keep going.
(/ō/, /ō/, roast;
/oi/, /oi/, join;
/ĭ/, /ĭ/, link;
/ā/, /ā/, gray . . .)

COMPREHENSION PROCESSES

Remember, Understand, Apply

PROCEDURES

1. Introducing the Magazine

Identifying—Title, What; Priming Background Knowledge

Have students identify the title of their magazine.

Say something like:

Today, we get to read the *Read Well Science Digest*.

It's really cool. It's a magazine.

What's the title of your magazine? (Read Well Science Digest)

Magazines are fun because they are full of short articles about interesting things.

Let's find out about some of the things you will read about.

Find "Food Chains." Read the first question about food chains.

(Where do meatballs come from?)

That question is called a cover line. It's written to get you interested in what's inside the magazine.

Do you know where meatballs come from? (supermarkets, the freezer, meat . . .)

That's right, but the answer might surprise you. So we'll have to read to see if the answer in the magazine does surprise us.

Read the next cover line. (Worms in the food chain! Yuck or yeah?)

So what else are we going to read about? (worms) Yuck? Or yeah? What do you think now? We'll see if you change your mind after you've read the magazine.

Read the next cover line . . .

2. Using the Table of Contents

Using the Table of Contents, Identifying—Titles

Have students look at the Table of Contents. Say something like:

Look at the Table of Contents on page 3. In magazines, the Table of Contents looks a little different, but it still helps us find out what we're going to read about and where it's located.

The first thing in the Table of Contents is a section about departments. The page number is listed first. Find the "Letter From the Editor." What page is it on? (page 5)

Find the word *features*. A feature article is a story in a magazine. What are some of the feature articles listed? (Links in the Chain, From Grass to Meatballs . . .)

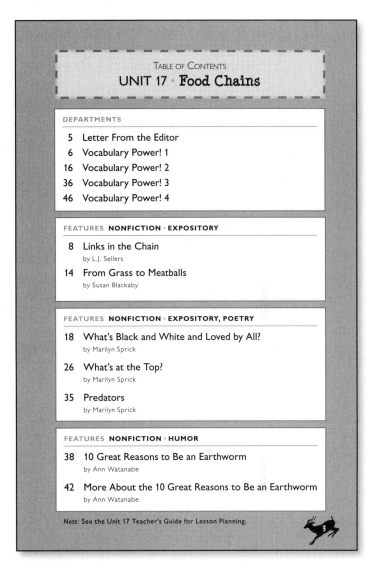

TABLE OF CONTENTS
UNIT 17 · Food Chains

DEPARTMENTS

5 Letter From the Editor
6 Vocabulary Power! 1
16 Vocabulary Power! 2
36 Vocabulary Power! 3
46 Vocabulary Power! 4

FEATURES NONFICTION · EXPOSITORY

8 Links in the Chain
by L.J. Sellers
14 From Grass to Meatballs
by Susan Blackaby

FEATURES NONFICTION · EXPOSITORY, POETRY

18 What's Black and White and Loved by All?
by Marilyn Sprick
26 What's at the Top?
by Marilyn Sprick
35 Predators
by Marilyn Sprick

FEATURES NONFICTION · HUMOR

38 10 Great Reasons to Be an Earthworm
by Ann Watanabe
42 More About the 10 Great Reasons to Be an Earthworm
by Ann Watanabe

Note: See the Unit 17 Teacher's Guide for Lesson Planning.

3. Introducing the Unit

Using the Table of Contents; Identifying—Titles, What; Viewing; Inferring

Have students look at the Table of Contents. Say something like:

Turn to page 4 of the Table of Contents.
What are you going to read on page 62?
(Links in a Food Chain)
Yes, you're going to read a poem called
"Links in a Food Chain."

Look at the photos in the circles. What do
you see in the circle at the bottom of the
page? (leaves and fruit)
What do you see in the next circle? (a bird,
a toucan)
That's right. The toucan eats the fruit.
Look at the next circle.
What do you see? (a snake)
What do you think the snake eats? (the
toucan)

That's right. The circles show a food chain,
and that's what this magazine, and this unit,
is all about.

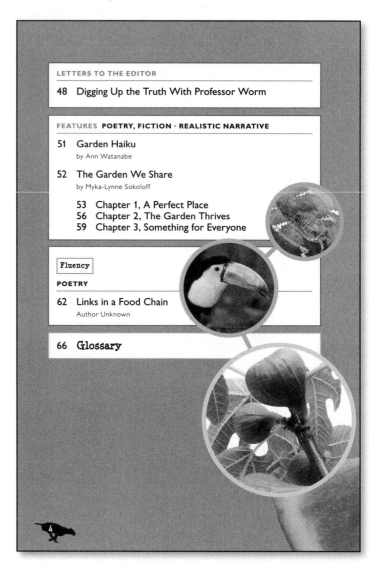

4. Introducing the Letter From the Editor

Identifying—Who

- Explain what an editor and a letter from the editor are. Say something like:

  Look at page 5. The first thing we're going to read today is the "Letter From the Editor."

  Who is the letter from? (the editor)

  The editor of a magazine is in charge of everything that goes in the magazine. In the "Letter From the Editor," the editor talks to the readers. Who is the editor talking to? (us, the readers)

  Look at the picture and the signature at the bottom of the letter. Who is the editor of this magazine? (Professor Worm)

  Interesting—with a worm in charge, this should be a fun magazine!

- Have students read the letter from the editor. Mix group and individual turns.

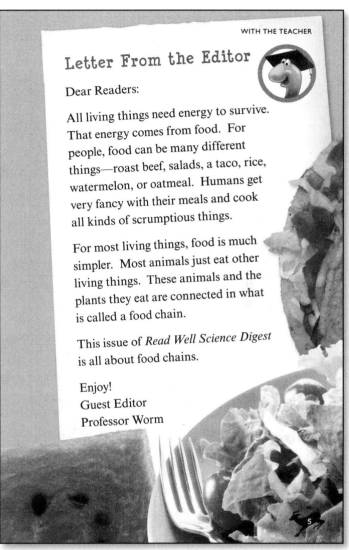

WITH THE TEACHER

Letter From the Editor

Dear Readers:

All living things need energy to survive. That energy comes from food. For people, food can be many different things—roast beef, salads, a taco, rice, watermelon, or oatmeal. Humans get very fancy with their meals and cook all kinds of scrumptious things.

For most living things, food is much simpler. Most animals just eat other living things. These animals and the plants they eat are connected in what is called a food chain.

This issue of *Read Well Science Digest* is all about food chains.

Enjoy!
Guest Editor
Professor Worm

5

After Reading Page 5

❶ **Understand:** Explaining
What did Professor Worm tell you about humans?
(They get fancy about the food they eat . . .)

❷ **Understand:** Explaining
What did Professor Worm say most animals do?
(They get their food by eating other animals, plants, living things . . .)

COMPREHENSION PROCESSES

Understand, Apply

PROCEDURES

Introducing Vocabulary

> ☆**energy** ☆**connect** ☆**link,**
> **herbivore, carnivore**

- For each vocabulary word, have students read the word by parts, then read the whole word.
- Read the student-friendly explanations to students as they follow with their fingers. Then have students use the vocabulary word by following the gray text.
- Review and discuss the photos.

USING VOCABULARY

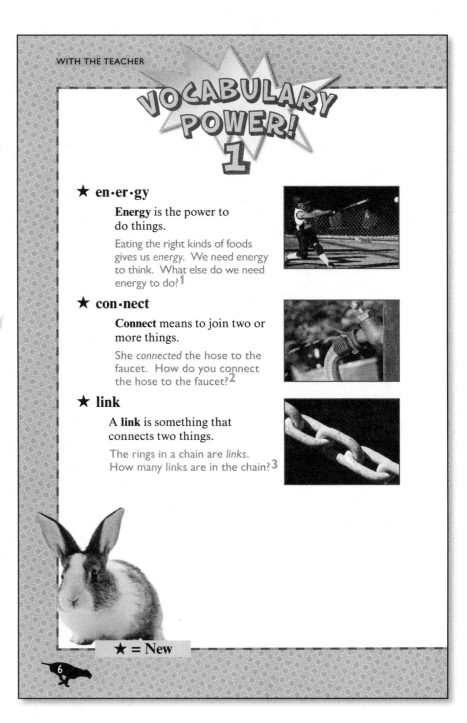

WITH THE TEACHER

VOCABULARY POWER! 1

★ **en·er·gy**

Energy is the power to do things.

Eating the right kinds of foods gives us *energy*. We need energy to think. What else do we need energy to do?[1]

★ **con·nect**

Connect means to join two or more things.

She *connected* the hose to the faucet. How do you connect the hose to the faucet?[2]

★ **link**

A **link** is something that connects two things.

The rings in a chain are *links*. How many links are in the chain?[3]

★ = New

6

---

[1] Apply: Making Connections; Using Vocabulary—energy (We need energy to play . . .)

[2] Apply: Priming Background Knowledge; Using Vocabulary—connect (You connect the hose to the faucet by screwing it on.)

[3] Apply: Using Vocabulary—link (There are five links in the chain.)

her·bi·vore

An **herbivore** is an animal that eats only plants.

A rabbit is an *herbivore.* What does a rabbit eat?[1]

car·ni·vore

A **carnivore** is an animal that eats mostly meat.

A wolf is a *carnivore.* What does a wolf eat?[2]

USING VOCABULARY

VOCABULARY REVIEW (Reminder)

Keep a running list of vocabulary words on the board, a chart, or in a pocket chart. Encourage students to use the words when they talk or write.

1 **Understand:** Defining and Using Vocabulary—herbivore (A rabbit is an herbivore, so it eats only plants.)

2 **Understand:** Defining and Using Vocabulary—carnivore (A wolf is a carnivore, so it eats mostly meat.)

"LINKS IN THE CHAIN" INSTRUCTIONS

Students read "Links in the Chain" on pages 8–13 with the teacher and "From Grass to Meatballs" on pages 14–15 on their own.

COMPREHENSION PROCESSES

Remember, Understand, Apply, Analyze

COMPREHENSION BUILDING

- Encourage students to answer questions with complete sentences.
- If students have difficulty comprehending, think aloud with them or reread the portion of the story that answers the question. Repeat the question.

PROCEDURES

1. **Introducing "Links in the Chain"**

   Identifying—Title, Author
   - Discuss the title and author. Say something like:

     What's the title of this article? (Links in the Chain)
     Who wrote the article? (L.J. Sellers) So L.J. Sellers is the . . . author.

2. **First Reading**
   - Ask questions and discuss the story as indicated by the gray text.
   - Mix group and individual turns, independent of your voice.
     Have students work toward a group accuracy goal of 0–2 errors.
     Quietly keep track of errors made by all students in the group.
   - After reading the story, practice any difficult words.
     Reread the story if students have not reached the accuracy goal.

3. **Second Reading, Short Passage Practice: Developing Prosody**
   - Demonstrate expressive, fluent reading of the first paragraph.
     Read at a rate slightly faster than the students' rate. Say something like:

     Listen to me as I read the first page.
     I'm going to read like I do as a teacher. I'm going to emphasize information that I think is important or interesting.

     "Food chains are everywhere. Grass grows in a meadow.
     A deer grazes on the grass. Then a cougar kills and eats the deer."

   - Guide practice with your voice.

     Read the first page with me—as if you were the teacher.

   - Provide individual turns while others track with their fingers and whisper read.
   - Repeat with one paragraph at a time. Repeat steps with each remaining paragraph.

> **REPEATED READINGS**
>
> **Prosody**
>
> On the second reading, students practice developing prosody— phrasing and expression. Research has shown that prosody is related to both fluency and comprehension.

WITH THE TEACHER

Links in the Chain

by L.J. Sellers

Food chains are everywhere.

Grass grows in a meadow.
A deer grazes on the grass.
Then a cougar kills and eats the deer.

8

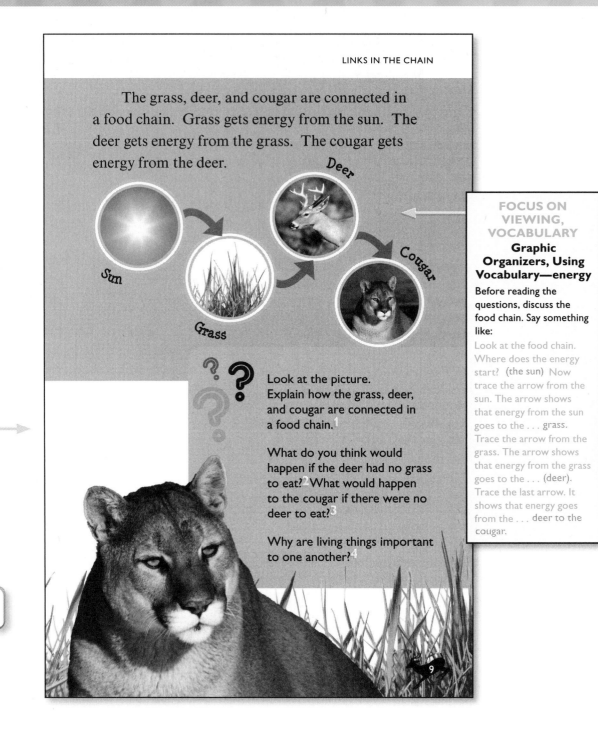

LINKS IN THE CHAIN

The grass, deer, and cougar are connected in a food chain. Grass gets energy from the sun. The deer gets energy from the grass. The cougar gets energy from the deer.

Deer

Cougar

Sun

Grass

Look at the picture. Explain how the grass, deer, and cougar are connected in a food chain.¹

What do you think would happen if the deer had no grass to eat?² What would happen to the cougar if there were no deer to eat?³

Why are living things important to one another?⁴

FOCUS ON VIEWING, VOCABULARY

Graphic Organizers, Using Vocabulary—energy

Before reading the questions, discuss the food chain. Say something like:

Look at the food chain. Where does the energy start? (the sun) Now trace the arrow from the sun. The arrow shows that energy from the sun goes to the . . . grass. Trace the arrow from the grass. The arrow shows that energy from the grass goes to the . . . (deer). Trace the last arrow. It shows that energy goes from the . . . deer to the cougar.

COMPREHENDING AS YOU GO

9

❶ **Understand:** Viewing; Explaining; Using Vocabulary—connect, energy (The grass gets energy from the sun. The deer gets energy by eating the grass. The cougar gets energy by eating the deer.)

❷ **Apply:** Inferring, Explaining (The deer would die if it had no grass to eat. The deer would go to where there is grass . . .)

❸ **Apply:** Inferring, Explaining (The cougar would die if there were no deer to eat. The cougar would have to eat something else . . .)

❹ **Understand:** Explaining; Using Vocabulary—survive (Living things depend on other living things to survive.)

WITH THE TEACHER

Green Plants

Green plants are the first link in the food chain. These plants are special because they make their own food. They use water, sunlight, and air to make the food they need.

Green plants are everywhere. There are millions, billions, and trillions of plants. This is a good thing, because animals eat lots and lots of plants.

Why are green plants important?1

Plant Eaters

Plant eaters are the second link in the food chain. They come in all shapes and sizes. Tiny brown rabbits, mid-size brown deer, and enormous gray elephants are all plant eaters. Plant eaters live in forests, grasslands, rain forests, and oceans. Plant eaters are called herbivores.

What is the same about all herbivores?2

10

COMPREHENDING AS YOU GO

① **Apply:** Inferring; Explaining; Using Vocabulary—link (Green plants are important because many animals eat them. They are the first link in the food chain. They make . . .)

② **Understand:** Defining and Using Vocabulary—herbivore (They all eat plants. Herbivores are all plant eaters . . .)

LINKS IN THE CHAIN

Meat Eaters

Meat eaters—like eagles, wolves, and sharks—are at the top of the food chain. They eat other animals and are called carnivores. But carnivores have to watch out too. Some carnivores eat other carnivores.

Why do carnivores have to watch out too?1

In an ocean food chain, tiny plants are eaten by fish. Then the fish may be eaten by a seal. The seal is a carnivore, but it may be eaten by a killer whale.

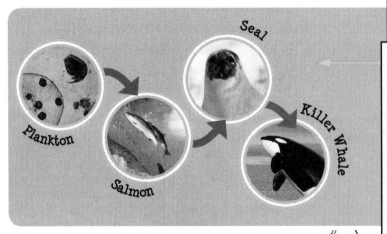

Seal

Plankton

Salmon

Killer Whale

11

COMPREHENDING AS YOU GO

FOCUS ON VIEWING, VOCABULARY

Graphic Organizers; Using Vocabulary— energy, link

After reading the page, say something like:
Look at the food chain. The energy starts with the sun. The sun filters through the water and goes to the plankton. Everyone touch the plankton.
Trace the arrow from the plankton to the next link. The arrow shows that energy from the plankton goes to the . . . (salmon). Trace the next arrow. It shows that energy goes from the . . . salmon to the seal. Finally, the last link is the . . . killer whale. What are all the links called? (a food chain)

① **Understand:** Explaining; Using Vocabulary—carnivore (A carnivore could be eaten by another carnivore.)

WITH THE TEACHER

A Food Chain Puzzle

Build a food chain from the following living things:
a cat, a caterpillar, a leaf, a robin.

Caterpillar

Cat

Leaf

Robin

1 Point to the first link in the food chain.[1]
2 Point to the second link.[2]
3 Point to the third link.[3]
4 Point to the fourth link. This animal is at the top of this food chain.[4]

Describe this food chain.[5]

12

COMPREHENDING AS YOU GO

❶ **Apply:** Demonstrate; Using Vocabulary—link
❷ **Apply:** Demonstrate; Using Vocabulary—link
❸ **Apply:** Demonstrate; Using Vocabulary—link
❹ **Apply:** Demonstrate; Using Vocabulary—link
❺ **Understand:** Describing, Summarizing (The caterpillar eats the leaf. The robin eats the caterpillar. The cat eats the robin.)

4. Introducing "Drain Your Brain"

Identifying—Title; Classifying; Using Vocabulary—link, food chain, herbivore, carnivore

- Discuss the title. Say something like:

  Read the title of this activity. (Drain Your Brain About the Chain)

  Note: If needed, remind students not to write in their books.

- Guide students as they determine what is right and not right.

  In "Drain Your Brain About the Chain," we're going to use our brains to figure out which sentences are *not* right.

  Look at the first picture.
  What do you see? (grass)
  Grass is the first . . . link in the food chain.

  Let's see if the first sentence about grass is *not* right.
  Read the sentence. (Herbivores love me.)
  Do herbivores love grass? (yes)
  Yes, many herbivores like to eat grass, so that sentence is right.

  Read the next sentence.
  (I get energy from the sun.)
  Does grass get energy from the sun? (yes)
  Correct! Grass gets energy from the sun, so that sentence is right.

  Read the last sentence. (I am a treat for carnivores.)
  Is grass a treat for carnivores? (no)
  Correct. Carnivores don't like to eat grass.
  You used your brains and figured out which sentence was not right.

  Carnivores don't eat grass. What do they eat? (meat)

- Repeat with the rabbit and the owl.

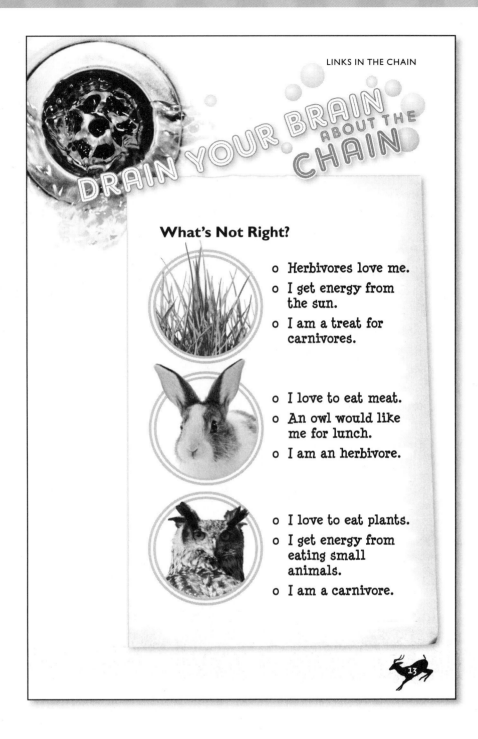

LINKS IN THE CHAIN

DRAIN YOUR BRAIN ABOUT THE CHAIN

What's Not Right?

o Herbivores love me.
o I get energy from the sun.
o I am a treat for carnivores.

o I love to eat meat.
o An owl would like me for lunch.
o I am an herbivore.

o I love to eat plants.
o I get energy from eating small animals.
o I am a carnivore.

13

"FROM GRASS TO MEATBALLS" INSTRUCTIONS

Students read pages 14 and 15 without the teacher, independently or with partners.

COMPREHENSION PROCESSES

Remember, Apply

PROCEDURES FOR READING ON YOUR OWN

1. **Getting Ready**

    Have students turn to "From Grass to Meatballs" on page 14.

2. **Setting a Purpose**

    Identifying—What; Explaining

    Before students begin reading, say something like:

    You're going to read the next article on your own.

    Read to find out the answers to these questions:

    - What food chain is described in the article?
    - Why should you say "Thank you" next time you see green grass?

3. **Reading on Your Own: Partner or Whisper Reading**

    - Have students take turns reading every other page with a partner or have students whisper read on their own.
    - Continue having students track each word with their fingers.

    For Whisper Reading, say something like:

    Everyone, turn to page 14. This is where you're going to start reading on your own—without me. Please whisper read with your finger, so I can see where you are in your work.

    You are going to stop reading at the end of page 15.

    For Partner Reading, say something like:

    Everyone, turn to page 14. This is where you're going to start Partner Reading.

    Where are you going to sit? (at our desks, side by side)

    You will take turns reading pages. If you are the listener, what will you do? (keep my book flat, follow with my finger, compliment my partner)

    If you are the reader, what will you do? (keep my book flat, finger track, read quietly)

    You are going to stop reading at the end of page 15.

4. **Comprehension and Skill Work**

    For students on a 6-Day Plan, tell them they will do Comprehension and Skill Activities 1 and 2 after they read on their own. Guide practice, as needed. For teacher directions, see pages 33 and 34.

5. **Homework 1: Repeated Reading**

> **PREP NOTE**
> **Setting a Purpose**
> Write questions on a chalkboard, white board, or large piece of paper before working with your small group.

ON YOUR OWN

From Grass to Meatballs

by Susan Blackaby

As the first link in the food chain, green plants are very important. Without green plants, there would be no meatballs. What? You say no meatballs! How can that be?

Follow the chain:

1 The grass makes food, using energy from the sun.

2 Cattle eat the grass.

14

FROM GRASS TO MEATBALLS

Without green plants, what would happen to your meatballs? Without grass, the cattle would starve. Without cattle, there would be no meat to package. Without meat, there would be no meatballs.

So the next time you see green grass in a field, think meatballs and say "Thank you."

3 The butcher packages and sells the meat.

4 You and your family make meatballs from a package of that meat.

Why are green plants needed for meatballs?

15

COMPREHENDING AS YOU GO

❶ **Understand:** Explaining, Summarizing (Meat for the meatballs comes from cattle. The cattle eat green plants. So without green plants, there would be no meat for the meatballs.)

PASSAGE COMPREHENSION

COMPREHENSION PROCESSES

Remember, Understand, Apply

WRITING TRAITS

Conventions—Period

Identifying—Fact
Using Vocabulary—energy

Using Vocabulary—connect, link

Using Graphic Organizer; Describing
Sequencing; Using Vocabulary—energy

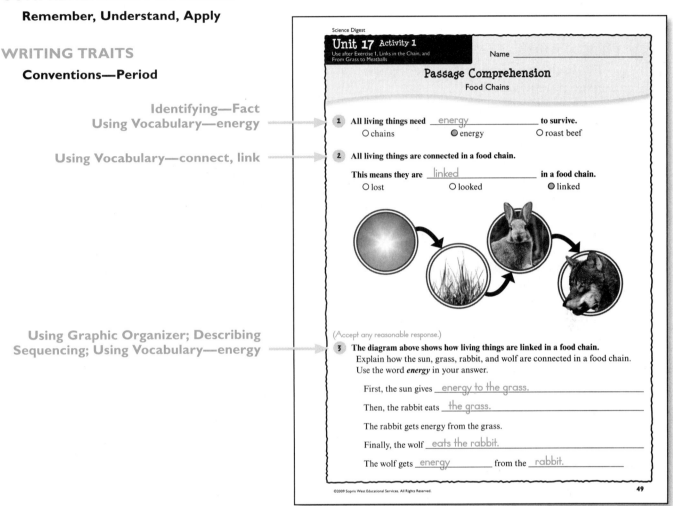

Science Digest

Unit 17 Activity 1
Use after Exercise 1, Links in the Chain, and
From Grass to Meatballs

Name _____

Passage Comprehension
Food Chains

1 All living things need ___energy___ to survive.
   ○ chains   ● energy   ○ roast beef

2 All living things are connected in a food chain.

This means they are ___linked___ in a food chain.
   ○ lost   ○ looked   ● linked

(Accept any reasonable response.)

3 The diagram above shows how living things are linked in a food chain.
Explain how the sun, grass, rabbit, and wolf are connected in a food chain.
Use the word *energy* in your answer.

First, the sun gives ___energy to the grass.___

Then, the rabbit eats ___the grass.___

The rabbit gets energy from the grass.

Finally, the wolf ___eats the rabbit.___

The wolf gets ___energy___ from the ___rabbit.___

    49

PROCEDURES

For each step, demonstrate and guide practice, as needed. Then have students complete the page independently.

1. **Selection Response—Basic Instructions** (Items 1, 2)
   Have students read each sentence, then fill in the bubble and/or blank with the correct answer.

2. **Diagram: Sentence Completion—Specific Instructions** (Item 3)
   Have students read Item 3 and trace the food chain in the diagram. Next, have students write phrases that correctly describe the food chain. Remind students to put a period at the end of each sentence.

Self-monitoring
Have students check and correct their work.

MAZE READING AND SEQUENCE • BUILD A FOOD CHAIN

COMPREHENSION PROCESSES
Understand, Apply

PROCEDURES
For each step, demonstrate and guide practice, as needed. Then have students complete the page independently.

1. **Maze Reading—Basic Instructions**
   - Have students read the sentences and circle the words in the parentheses that make the most sense.
   - Then have students read the sentences with their word choices to see if they make sense.

2. **Sequence Chart: Illustrating—Specific Instructions**
   - Have students read the directions. Then have students complete the food chain by filling in the blanks. Have students look in their storybooks and/or brainstorm possible answers, as needed. Say something like:

     Look at the first row. First, there's the sun. The energy from the sun flows to a . . . plant.
     What are some plants that you might write in the first blank? (grass, leaf, wheat, lettuce, flowers, berries . . .)
     Let's think about using berries for the plant in this food chain.

     Next, the arrow shows that energy from the plant goes to an . . . (herbivore).
     Name some herbivores that eat berries. (mice, deer . . .)
     That's right. Deer are herbivores and so are some mice. Let's think about using a rabbit for the herbivore in this food chain.

     Read the word below the next link in the food chain. (carnivore)
     Name some carnivores that might eat a mouse. (eagle, owl, fox, cat . . .)
     That's right. We could use any of those carnivores to complete the food chain.

   - Have students write their choices in the blanks and then illustrate their own food chain.

Comprehension Monitoring, Test Taking

Using Graphic Organizer; Sequencing Defining and/or Using Vocabulary—food chain, herbivore, carnivore; Illustrating

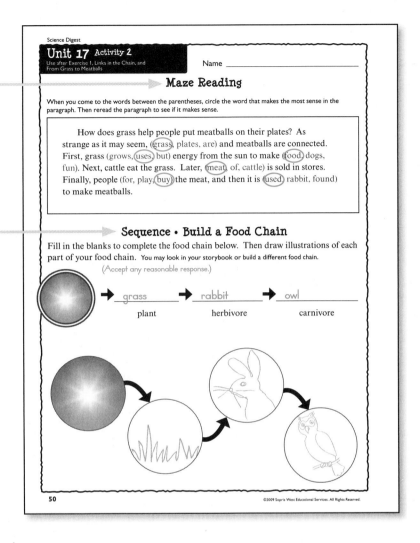

Science Digest

Unit 17 Activity 2
Use after Exercise 1, Links in the Chain, and From Grass to Meatballs

Name _____

Maze Reading

When you come to the words between the parentheses, circle the word that makes the most sense in the paragraph. Then reread the paragraph to see if it makes sense.

How does grass help people put meatballs on their plates? As strange as it may seem, (grass, plates, are) and meatballs are connected. First, grass (grows, uses, but) energy from the sun to make (food, dogs, fun). Next, cattle eat the grass. Later, (meat, of, cattle) is sold in stores. Finally, people (for, play, buy) the meat, and then it is (used, rabbit, found) to make meatballs.

Sequence • Build a Food Chain

Fill in the blanks to complete the food chain below. Then draw illustrations of each part of your food chain. You may look in your storybook or build a different food chain.

(Accept any reasonable response.)

grass → rabbit → owl

plant   herbivore   carnivore

1 SOUND REVIEW

2 ACCURACY AND FLUENCY BUILDING

> **ACCURACY AND FLUENCY PROCEDURES**
> - For each task, have students say any underlined part, then read the word.
> - Set a pace. Then have students read the whole words in each task and column.
> - Provide repeated practice, building accuracy first, then fluency.

C1. Multisyllabic Words

- For the list of words divided by syllables, have students read each syllable, then the whole word. Use the word in a sentence, as appropriate.
- For the list of whole words, build accuracy and then fluency.

recognize	He didn't know who I was. He didn't . . . *recognize* . . . me.
intelligent	You are a smart class! You are all very . . . *intelligent.*
muscular	The athlete had a lot of muscles. She was . . . *muscular.*
difference	Eating right makes a . . . *difference.*
mistakes	I read carefully so I don't make any . . . *mistakes.*
single	There weren't any pens left. There wasn't a . . . *single* . . . one.
eyesight	Eagles have very good . . . *eyesight.*
meantime	We have time before the show starts. Let's eat in the . . . *meantime.*

D1. Tricky Words

- For each Tricky Word, have students use the sounds and word parts they know to silently sound out the word. Use the word in a sentence to help with pronunciation.
- If the word is unfamiliar, tell students the word.

unique

Look at the first word. The word is *unique*. Say the word. (unique)

If there's only one of something, it is special and . . . *unique.*

Read the word three times. (unique, unique, unique)

scarce

Look at the next word. Sound out the word silently. Thumbs up when you know the word.

Use my sentence to help you pronounce the word. In the winter, food became . . . *scarce.*

Read the word three times. (scarce, scarce, scarce)

warning	When James saw Violet start to step in the mud, he yelled out a . . . *warning.*
course	I'm definitely going to the party. Of . . . *course* . . . I will be there.

3 WORDS IN CONTEXT

4 MORPHOGRAPHS AND AFFIXES

⭐In Row A, introduce and practice the affix *-ity*. Say something like:

You can already read your new affix. Sound it out. (/ĭĭĭty/, *-ity*)

What's the affix say? (*-ity*) Read the underlined affix and then each whole word. (*-ity*, activity . . .)

- In Row B, have students read each affix and then the whole word. For the word "powerful," review the meaning of the morphograph. Say something like:

Powerful means full of . . . (power).

5 GENERALIZATION: READING NEW WORDS IN PARAGRAPHS

- Have students read the paragraph silently, then out loud. Tell students to use the sounds and word parts they know to read any difficult words.
- Repeat practice, as needed.

⭐ = New in this unit

Science Digest

Unit 17 Exercise 2

Use before What's Black and White and Loved by All? and What's at the Top?

1. SOUND REVIEW Have students review sounds for accuracy, then for fluency.

A	ou	aw	-dge	au	oy
B	ge	ph	ci	gi	kn

2. ACCURACY/FLUENCY BUILDING For each column, have students say any underlined part, then read each word. Next, have them read the column.

A1 Mixed Practice	**B1** Word Endings	**C1** Multisyllabic Words		**D1** Tricky Words
poun<u>ce</u>	whuffle	re•cog•nize	recognize	unique
bra<u>y</u>	whuffling	in•tel•li•gent	intelligent	scarce
<u>qu</u>iz		mus•cu•lar	muscular	warning
r<u>oa</u>rs	whinny	dif•fer•ence	difference	course
me<u>ows</u>	whinnies	mis•takes	mistakes	
sn<u>ar</u>ls		sin•gle	single	
b<u>ea</u>sts	bite	eye•sight	eyesight	
pr<u>i</u>de	biting	mean•time	meantime	
gra<u>z</u>ers				

BUILDING MASTERY (Reminder)

For each task, have students work first on accuracy, then on fluency. Have fun! Practice words multiple times in varied ways. Have students whisper the words, squeak the words, and read the sounds and words in a rhythm.

3. WORDS IN CONTEXT Have students use the sounds and word parts they know to figure out the word. Then have students read the sentence.

A	ser•i•ous	Zack was not joking. He was very <u>serious</u>.
B	wrest•ling	The cubs were <u>wrestling</u> and playing while the lazy lioness snoozed.
C	pred•a•tors	Lions are <u>predators</u>. Zebras and impalas are often their prey.
D	e•nough	We had more than <u>enough</u> to eat. Our bellies were stuffed!

GENTLE CORRECTIONS

If you hear an error, write the word on the board.

Have all students identify the difficult sound and then blend the word.

Periodically, repeat practice of the difficult word.

4. MORPHOGRAPHS AND AFFIXES Have students practice reading "-ity" and the related words. For Row B, have students read the underlined part, then the word.

A	★ -ity	activ<u>ity</u>	commun<u>ity</u>	abil<u>ity</u>	responsibil<u>ity</u>
B	power<u>ful</u>	protec<u>tion</u>	<u>defend</u>	noma<u>dic</u>	<u>ex</u>plore

5. GENERALIZATION: Have students read the paragraph silently, then out loud. (New words: hyenas, impalas, stripes)

Our field trip to the zoo was amazing. We saw giraffes, hyenas, impalas, antelopes, and crocodiles. We sat in front of the zebras and drew some pictures. We noticed that each zebra had a different pattern of stripes.

37

COMPREHENSION PROCESSES

Understand, Apply

PROCEDURES

1. Introducing Vocabulary

> ☆ **unique, predator**
> ☆ **nomadic, scarce, prey**
> ☆ **food chain**

- For each vocabulary word, have students read the word by parts, then read the whole word.
- Read the student-friendly explanations to students as they follow with their fingers. Then have students use the vocabulary word by following the gray text.
- Review and discuss the photos and illustrations.

USING VOCABULARY

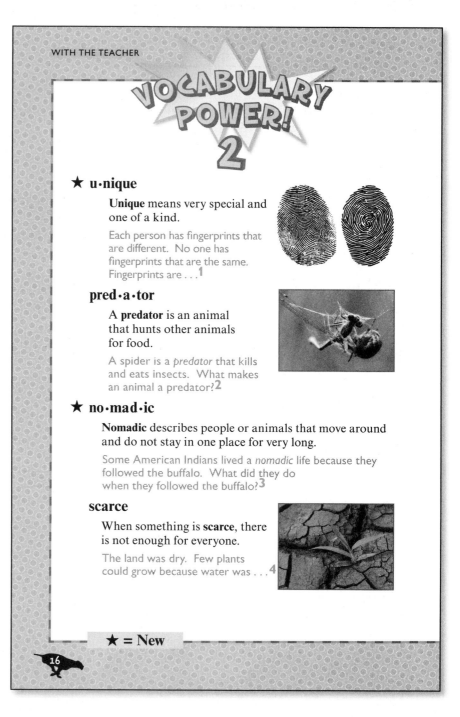

WITH THE TEACHER

VOCABULARY POWER! 2

★ **u·nique**

Unique means very special and one of a kind.

Each person has fingerprints that are different. No one has fingerprints that are the same. Fingerprints are . . .**1**

pred·a·tor

A **predator** is an animal that hunts other animals for food.

A spider is a *predator* that kills and eats insects. What makes an animal a predator?**2**

★ **no·mad·ic**

Nomadic describes people or animals that move around and do not stay in one place for very long.

Some American Indians lived a *nomadic* life because they followed the buffalo. What did they do when they followed the buffalo?**3**

scarce

When something is **scarce**, there is not enough for everyone.

The land was dry. Few plants could grow because water was . . .**4**

★ = New

16

---

❶ Understand: Defining and Using Vocabulary—unique (unique)

❷ Understand: Defining and Using Vocabulary—predator (An animal that kills and eats other animals for food is a predator.)

❸ Understand: Defining Vocabulary—nomadic (When they followed the buffalo, they moved around and didn't stay in one place for very long.)

❹ Apply: Using Vocabulary—scarce (scarce)

☆ = New in this unit

2. Now You Try It!

- Read or paraphrase the directions.
- Then, for each word, have students read the word by parts and then read the whole word.
- Have students explain or define the word in their own words. Say something like:

  Look at the first word under Now You Try It. Say the parts, then read the whole word. (food chain) Now let's pretend that we're going to explain or define the word *food chain* to a friend. [Barry], what would you say?

  Start with "A *food chain* is . . . " (A food chain is when one thing eats another.)

  Excellent. [Arthur], how would you explain or define the word *food chain*? (A food chain is about plants, plant eaters, and meat eaters.)

  Yes, that's right. In a food chain, plants are eaten by plant eaters—called . . . herbivores. Then the herbivores are eaten by . . . carnivores.

- Have students turn to the appropriate page in the glossary and discuss how their definitions are the same as or different from the glossary's. Your students may like their definitions better.

Note: By defining a word in their own words, students are demonstrating depth of word knowledge. Verbatim responses only demonstrate memorization. Encourage paraphrasing.

WHAT'S BLACK AND WHITE AND LOVED BY ALL?

prey

Prey is an animal that is hunted and eaten by another animal.

Rabbits are the *prey* of wolves and other carnivores. What are other kinds of prey?[1]

Now You Try It!
Try defining the next word. Then look up the word in the glossary. Your definition might be better!

★ **food chain**

Start with "A *food chain* is . . ."[2] Let's find the word on page 67.

USING VOCABULARY

17

❶ **Apply:** Using Vocabulary—prey (An insect is a spider's prey.)

❷ **Understand:** Defining and Using Vocabulary—food chain, link; Using Glossary (A food chain is how plants and animals are linked together in a chain . . .)

"WHAT'S BLACK AND WHITE?" INSTRUCTIONS

Students read "What's Black and White and Loved By All?" on pages 18–25 with the teacher. Students read "What's at the Top?" on pages 26–35 on their own during their independent work.

Note: If you're working on an 8- to 11-Day Plan, you will read "What's at the Top?" with students.

COMPREHENSION PROCESSES

Remember, Understand, Apply, Evaluate

PROCEDURES

1. **Reviewing "From Grass to Meatballs"**

   Identifying—Facts; Describing; Explaining; Using Vocabulary—food chain, link
   Discuss the questions from Setting a Purpose. Say something like:
   Yesterday, you read "From Grass to Meatballs" on your own. Let's see what you found out.
   What food chain is described in the article?
   (The first link in the food chain is the grass. The next link in the food chain is the cattle.
   The cattle is made into meat, and then people make meatballs from the meat . . .)
   Why should you say "Thank you" next time you see green grass?
   (Without the grass, we wouldn't have meatballs to eat . . .)

2. **Introducing "What's Black and White and Loved by All?"**

   Identifying—Title, Author; Inferring
   Discuss the title and clues about the article. Say something like:
   What's the title of this article? (What's Black and White and Loved by All?)
   Who is Marilyn Sprick? (She is the author.)
   Everyone, read what it says in the first speech bubble.
   (What's black and white and smiles?) Now read the next speech bubble.
   (What's black and white and makes whuffling sounds?)
   Look at the pictures. What's in the first picture? (a panda)
   Is it black and white? (yes) Does it smile? (maybe)
   Do you think it makes a whuffling sound? (not sure)
   Do you know what a whuffling sound is?
   It's a "whuh, whuh, whuh, whuh, whuh, whuh" sound.
   Do you think this article is about a panda?
   Repeat as appropriate with the other pictures and then vote.

3. **First Reading**
   - Ask questions and discuss the story as indicated by the gray text.
   - Mix group and individual turns, independent of your voice.
     Have students work toward a group accuracy goal of 0–2 errors.
   - After reading the story, practice any difficult words. Reread the story if students have not reached the accuracy goal.

4. **Second Reading, Short Passage Practice: Developing Prosody**
   - Demonstrate how to read a paragraph with expression.
   - Have students read the paragraph with you.
   - Have individuals read the paragraph with expression.

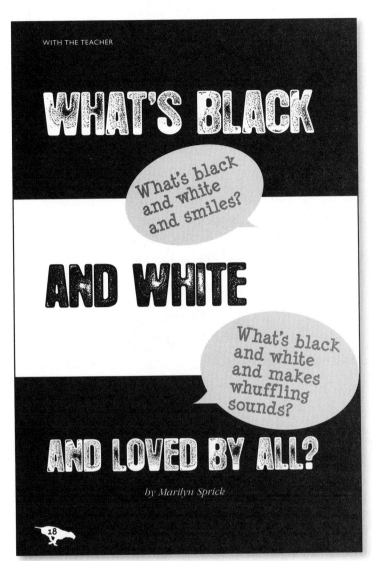

It's a Zebra!

A zebra is in the horse family. Like a horse, a zebra whinnies, grazes, and runs like the wind. Zebras also bray and make strange snorting, whuffling sounds. Of course, a zebra is black and white and has stripes.

20

WHAT'S BLACK AND WHITE AND LOVED BY ALL?

What's With the Stripes?

Every zebra has its own pattern of stripes. Zebras use these unique patterns to recognize one another. Look carefully. Can you tell the difference between the two zebras? What is unique about each zebra's stripes?

Name three facts about a zebra. 1

21

COMPREHENDING AS YOU GO

❶ **Remember:** Identifying—Facts; **Understand:** Using Vocabulary—unique (A zebra is in the horse family. A zebra makes snorting, whuffling sounds. A zebra has a unique pattern of stripes . . .)

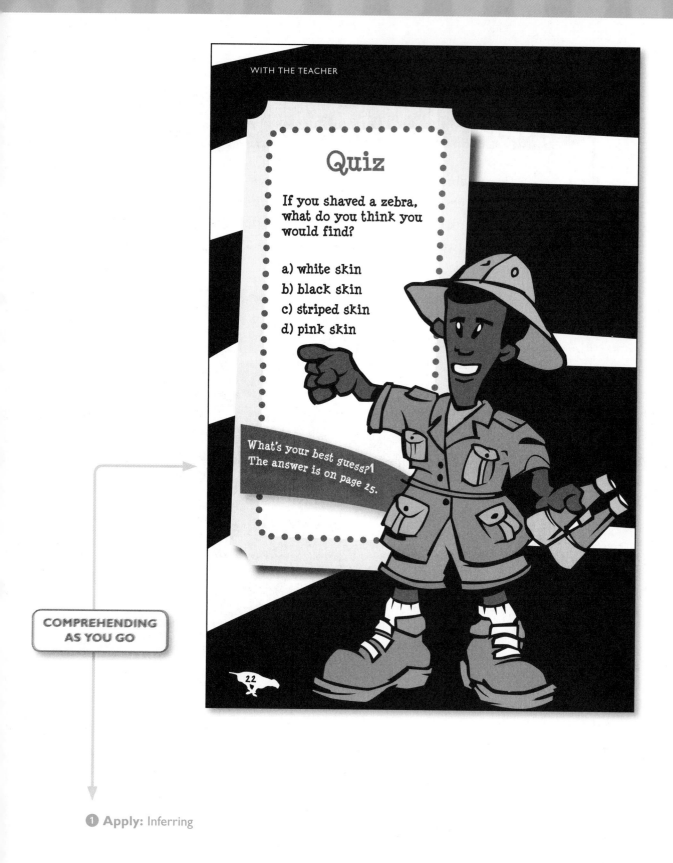

WITH THE TEACHER

Quiz

If you shaved a zebra, what do you think you would find?

a) white skin
b) black skin
c) striped skin
d) pink skin

What's your best guess?❶
The answer is on page 25.

22

COMPREHENDING
AS YOU GO

❶ **Apply:** Inferring

Zebras in the Food Chain

Grass is the first link in the zebra's food chain. Zebras are the second link. They are nomadic herbivores. They travel around in search of fresh grass and water.

Lions are the next link in the food chain. These carnivores wait at the water holes for the zebras. Zebras know when lions are nearby, but water is often scarce and the zebras must drink.

Zebra Food Chains

Zebra's main predators are lions, hyenas, and crocodiles.

At the water hole, which animal is the predator?1 Which is the prey?2

23

FOCUS ON VIEWING, VOCABULARY

Graphic Organizers, Using Vocabulary—energy, link, connect, predator, prey

After completing the page, say something like:
Look at the food chain. The energy starts with the sun. What gets energy from the sun? (the grass) That's right. Trace the grass with your finger to the next link. How is the zebra connected to the grass? (The zebra eats the grass.) Trace the arrow from the zebra to the crocodile. How is the zebra connected to the crocodile? (The crocodile will eat a zebra.) That's right. The crocodile is the predator. What is its prey? (the zebra) What are the other predators in this food chain? (the lion and the hyena)

COMPREHENDING AS YOU GO

❶ **Analyze:** Classifying; **Apply:** Using Vocabulary—predator (The predators are the lions, hyenas, and crocodiles.)

❷ **Analyze:** Classifying; **Apply:** Using Vocabulary—prey (The zebra is the prey.)

WITH THE TEACHER

Protection

At the water hole, zebras must watch for predators, and they do. They must listen, and they do. When a lion is near, all the animals at the water hole must be on the lookout.

If zebras spot a lion, what should they do?1

24

COMPREHENDING AS YOU GO

❶ **Evaluate:** Making Judgments; **Apply:** Explaining (The zebras should run away. The zebras should hide . . .)

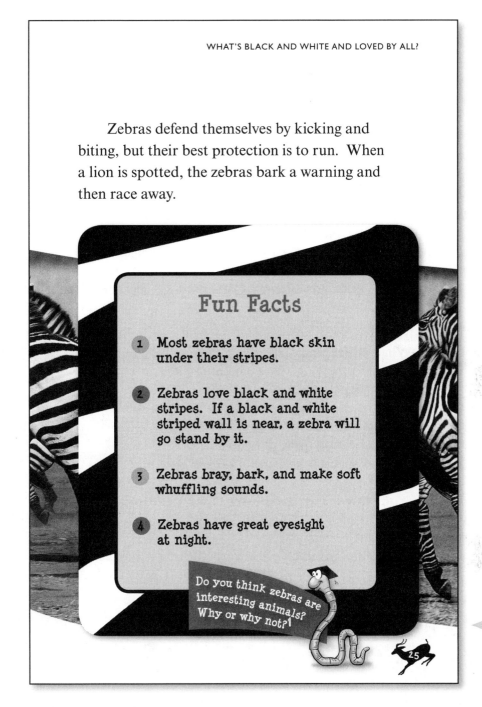

WHAT'S BLACK AND WHITE AND LOVED BY ALL?

Zebras defend themselves by kicking and biting, but their best protection is to run. When a lion is spotted, the zebras bark a warning and then race away.

Fun Facts

1 Most zebras have black skin under their stripes.

2 Zebras love black and white stripes. If a black and white striped wall is near, a zebra will go stand by it.

3 Zebras bray, bark, and make soft whuffling sounds.

4 Zebras have great eyesight at night.

Do you think zebras are interesting animals? Why or why not?[1]

25

COMPREHENDING
AS YOU GO

① **Evaluate:** Responding (Yes, zebras are interesting animals. I like their stripes. No, I would rather learn about a crocodile . . .)

"WHAT'S AT THE TOP?" INSTRUCTIONS

Students read "What's at the Top?" on pages 26–35 without the teacher, independently or with partners.

Note: If you're working on a lesson plan that is eight days or longer, you will read this chapter with your students.

COMPREHENSION PROCESSES

Remember, Understand, Apply, Evaluate

PROCEDURES FOR READING ON YOUR OWN

1. Getting Ready

Have students turn to page 26.

On page 26, you're going to start reading the next article in your magazine.

What's the title of the article? (What's at the Top?)

Look at the pictures. What do you think it is? (a lion, a tiger, a house cat . . .)

2. Setting a Purpose

Identifying—What; Describing; Explaining; Making Judgments

Establish a purpose for reading. Say something like:

Read to find out the answers to these questions:

- What is at the top of the food chain? Describe the food chain.
- How does this animal hunt for its prey?
- How do the baby animals learn to hunt?
- Do you think this animal is intelligent? Why or why not?

> **PREP NOTE**
>
> **Setting a Purpose**
>
> Write questions on a chalkboard, white board, or large piece of paper before working with your small group.

3. Reading on Your Own: Partner or Whisper Reading

- Have students take turns reading every other page with a partner or have students whisper read on their own.
- Continue having students track each word with their fingers.

For Whisper Reading, say something like:

Everyone, turn to page 26. This is where you're going to start reading on your own—without me. Please whisper read with your finger, so I can see where you are in your work.

You are going to stop reading at the end of page 35.

For Partner Reading, say something like:

Everyone, turn to page 26. This is where you're going to start Partner Reading.

Where are you going to sit? (at our desks, side by side)

You will take turns reading pages. If you are the listener, what will you do?

(keep my book flat, follow with my finger, compliment my partner)

If you are the reader, what will you do? (keep my book flat, finger track, read quietly)

You are going to stop reading at the end of page 35.

4. Comprehension and Skill Work

For students on a 6-Day Plan, tell them they will do Comprehension and Skill Activities 3 and 4 after they read on their own. Guide practice, as needed. For teacher directions, see pages 58 and 59. (For 8- to 11-Day Plans, see the Lesson Planner, page 9.)

5. Homework 2: Repeated Reading

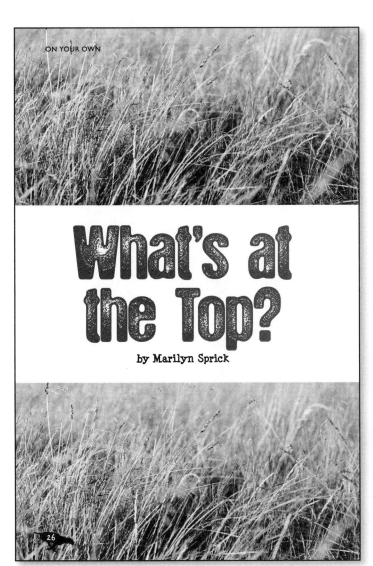

ON YOUR OWN

What's at the Top?

by Marilyn Sprick

26

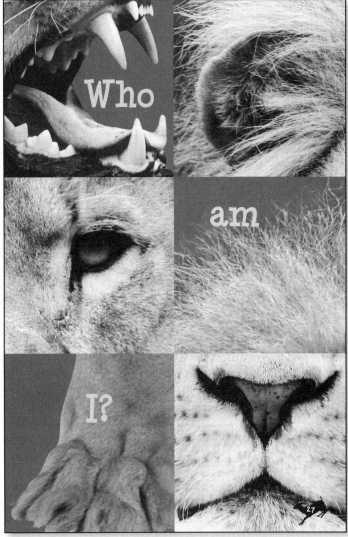

Who am I?

27

ON YOUR OWN

A Lion!

A lion is in the cat family. It meows. It hisses.
It snarls and roars. When a lion roars, it can be
heard from five miles away. A lion is at the top of the
food chain. He is often called the king of beasts.

Why is a lion
called the
king of beasts?1

28

**COMPREHENDING
AS YOU GO**

❶ **Apply:** Inferring; Explaining; Using Vocabulary—food chain (A lion is called the king of beasts because it is at
the top of the food chain.)

WHAT'S AT THE TOP?

Lions in the Food Chain

On the African grasslands, lions are at the top of the food chain. The grazers—zebras, impalas, buffalo, and giraffes—eat plants. Then these herbivores are food for the lions.

Quiz

If you were a lion, would you:

a) hunt all day?
b) take short naps?
c) sleep 21 hours a day?
d) go to the movies?

The answer is on page 34.

29

51

ON YOUR OWN

Teamwork

Lions live in families called prides. When the pride is hungry, the female cats hunt. At night or in the early morning, the big cats go in search of large mammals—buffalo, zebras, or antelopes.

When a lioness spots a herd of animals, for example, she huffs to let the others know. The other lionesses quickly crouch down. They move through the dry grass, closer and closer to their prey.

What is a lion family called?[1]
How does a lioness communicate with other lionesses during a hunt?[2]

30

COMPREHENDING AS YOU GO

[1] **Remember:** Identifying—What (A lion family is called a pride.)
[2] **Understand:** Explaining; Using Vocabulary—communicate (A lioness communicates by huffing to let the other lionesses know that a herd of animals is near.)

WHAT'S AT THE TOP?

When they get close to the herd, some of the lionesses move into the open. Members of the herd see the big cats and warn the others.

In the meantime, other lionesses move behind the herd. From behind, these cats pounce.

While the other animals in the herd run for their lives, the lionesses work together to bring down a single animal. Within minutes, the lions have a meal.

Explain how the lionesses use teamwork to bring down their prey.1

31

COMPREHENDING
AS YOU GO

❶ **Understand:** Explaining (Some lionesses move into the open so their prey can see them. Other lionesses move behind the herd and pounce.)

ON YOUR OWN

Learning to Hunt

When lion cubs are young, they play. They explore. They crouch. They pounce. They wrestle. In this way, the young lions learn the skills they need for hunting.

Once the lions are more than a year old, they go on hunts with their mothers. By age two, the lions are hunting small animals. At first, they make many mistakes. It is hard for the young lions to wait. The young lions often strike too soon, and their meals run away!

But lions are intelligent. They learn from their mistakes, and they watch their mothers. Before long, the young lions are helping feed their pride.

Name three ways a lion cub learns to hunt.1

What makes lions intelligent animals?2

32

COMPREHENDING AS YOU GO

① **Understand:** Summarizing—Facts (Young cubs play with each other and learn skills they need for hunting. Then they go hunting with their mothers. When they are two, they hunt on their own and learn from their mistakes.)

② **Apply:** Inferring, Explaining (Lions are intelligent because they learn from their mistakes and from watching their mothers.)

WHAT'S AT THE TOP?

A Cub's First Growl

Cubs Wrestling

A Cub Crouching

33

ON YOUR OWN

What Do Lions Do Best of All?

Lions are great sleepers. Lions sleep most of the day and night. In fact, lions may sleep as many as 21 hours in one day. That means these lazy cats may be awake for only three hours. A good snooze is what they do the best!

Name five interesting facts you learned about lions.1 What fact was the most interesting of all?2 This article says that lions are intelligent. Do you agree or disagree? Why?3

34

COMPREHENDING AS YOU GO

❶ **Understand:** Summarizing—Facts (Lions sleep most of the time. Lions work together to catch prey. Lions live in families called prides. Lions are at the top of the food chain. Lion cubs learn hunting skills by playing with each other . . .)

❷ **Evaluate:** Responding (The most interesting fact is that lionesses communicate with each other when they are hunting.)

❸ **Evaluate:** Making Judgments; **Apply:** Using Vocabulary—communicate (I think lions are intelligent because they communicate and are able to learn things. I don't think lions are intelligent because they are lazy and sleep all day.)

WHAT'S AT THE TOP?

Predators

Powerful bodies,
muscular legs,
intelligent animals
hunting their prey.

Top of the food chain,
bellies full,
serious sleepers
getting their rest.

—Marilyn Sprick

35

FACT SUMMARY

COMPREHENSION PROCESSES

Understand, Apply

WRITING TRAITS

Ideas and Content
Organization—Topic Sentence,
Supporting Details
Word Choice
Conventions—Complete Sentence,
Capital, Period
Presentation

Using Graphic Organizer
Summarizing—Facts
Locating Information

Summarizing—Main Idea/Topic,
Supporting Details/Facts
Using Vocabulary—mammal

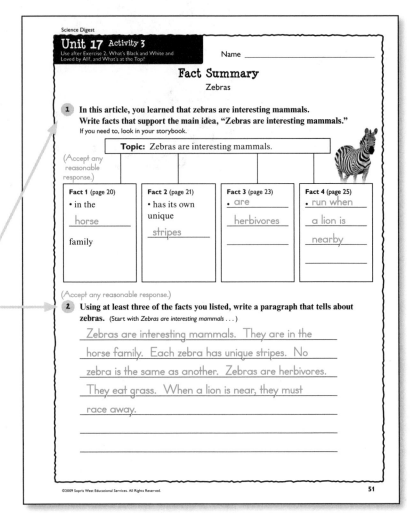

PROCEDURES

For each step, demonstrate and guide
practice, as needed. Then have students complete the page independently.

1. **Main Idea/Supporting Details: Hierarchy Chart, Sentence Completion—Specific Instructions** (Item 1)
   - Have students read the directions and discuss the graphic organizer. Say something like:
     Look at the top box of the graphic organizer. What was the article about? (zebras)
     Yes, so *zebras* are the topic of this organizer. The whole article described how zebras are interesting mammals, so "Zebras are interesting mammals" is a main idea of the article.

     Look in the smaller boxes. The smaller boxes are where we will complete the facts that tell us zebras are interesting mammals. Touch the first small box. Read and complete the first fact.

   - Repeat for each fact, as appropriate.

2. **Fact Summary: Paragraph Writing—Basic Instructions** (Item 2)
   - Have students read the instructions and write a paragraph using at least three facts from the graphic organizer.
   - Encourage students to add details and snazzy words.
   - Remind them to start sentences with a capital and end with a period.

PASSAGE COMPREHENSION

COMPREHENSION PROCESSES

Apply, Analyze

Using Graphic Organizer, Identifying—Facts; Test Taking

Using Graphic Organizer; Classifying Using Vocabulary—carnivore, energy, herbivore

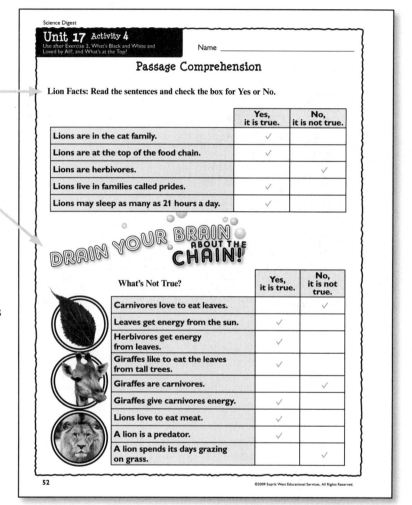

Science Digest

Unit 17 Activity 4
Use after Exercise 2, What's Black and White and Loved by All?, and What's at the Top?

Name _____

Passage Comprehension

Lion Facts: Read the sentences and check the box for Yes or No.

	Yes, it is true.	No, it is not true.
Lions are in the cat family.	✓	
Lions are at the top of the food chain.	✓	
Lions are herbivores.		✓
Lions live in families called prides.	✓	
Lions may sleep as many as 21 hours a day.	✓	

DRAIN YOUR BRAIN ABOUT THE CHAIN!

What's Not True?	Yes, it is true.	No, it is not true.
Carnivores love to eat leaves.		✓
Leaves get energy from the sun.	✓	
Herbivores get energy from leaves.	✓	
Giraffes like to eat the leaves from tall trees.	✓	
Giraffes are carnivores.		✓
Giraffes give carnivores energy.	✓	
Lions love to eat meat.	✓	
A lion is a predator.	✓	
A lion spends its days grazing on grass.		✓

52

PROCEDURES

For each step, demonstrate and guide practice, as needed. Then have students complete the page independently.

Lion Facts
True/Not True: Selection Response—Specific Instructions
Have students read each statement, determine if it is true or *not* true, then check the correct box. Say something like:

We are going to read sentences about lions. Some of the sentences are true, and some are *not* true. Read the first sentence. (Lions are in the cat family.)

Is this sentence true or not true? (true)

Yes, it is true. In the article, we learned that lions are in the cat family.

Which box will you check? (Yes, it is true.)

Guide students through the remainder of the sentences, as needed.

Drain Your Brain About the Chain
True/Not True: Selection Response—Specific Instructions
Have students look at each picture, read the sentences next to the picture, then check the sentence that is not true. Say something like:

Put your finger on the title "Drain Your Brain About the Chain."

Read the question under this title. (What's Not True?)

You're going to read sentences about each picture.

Some of the sentences are true, and some are not true.

Look at the first picture. What is that a picture of? (leaves)

Read the first sentence. (Carnivores love to eat leaves.) Is that true about leaves? (no)

That's correct, so which will you check? (No, it is not true.)

Guide students through the remainder of the pictures and sentences, as needed.

1 SOUND REVIEW

Use selected Sound Cards from Units 1–17.

PACING

Exercise 3a should take about 10 minutes to accommodate the Focus Lesson.

2 SHIFTY WORDS

For each word, have students say the underlined sound. Then have them sound out the word smoothly and say it.

3 ACCURACY AND FLUENCY BUILDING

- For each task, have students say any underlined part, then read the word.
- Set a pace. Then have students read the whole words in each task and column.
- Provide repeated practice, building accuracy first, then fluency.

B1. Related Words

- Have students read each word set.

☆ After reading each set, introduce the term "base word." Say something like:

The words *health*, *healthy*, and *healthier* are all related to one small word. The small word is called the base word. In this set of words, *health* is the base word.

Which word is the base word? (health)

D2. Rhyming Words

Have students read the rhyming words and identify what's the same about them.

E1. Tricky Words

- For each Tricky Word, have students use the sounds and word parts they know to silently sound out the word. Use the word in a sentence to help with pronunciation.

blood	The nurse cleaned my cut and wiped off the . . . *blood.*
hearts	Eden filled her valentine envelope with candy . . . *hearts.*
breaks	Be careful when you handle the egg. The shell easily . . . *breaks.*
wormy	The soil was full of worms. It was very . . . *wormy.*
answer	Jon raised his hand because he knew the . . . *answer.*

- Have students go back and read the whole words in the column.

4 WORDS IN CONTEXT

For each word, have students use the sounds and word parts they know to silently sound out the word. Then have students read the sentence. Assist, as needed.

5 MORPHOGRAPHS AND AFFIXES

- Have students read the underlined part, then the word.
- Repeat practice with whole words, mixing group and individual turns.
- For the word "recycle," review the meaning of the morphograph.
  Say something like: What does *re-* mean? (again) *Recycle* means to cycle or go around . . . again.

6 GENERALIZATION: READING NEW WORDS IN PARAGRAPHS

- Have students read the paragraph silently, then out loud. Tell students to use the sounds and word parts they know to read any difficult words.
- Repeat practice, as necessary.

☆ = New in this unit

Science Digest

Unit 17 Exercise 3a.
Use before Exercise 3b (Focus Lesson)

1. **SOUND REVIEW** Use selected Sound Cards from Units 1–17.

2. **SHIFTY WORD BLENDING** For each word, have students say the underlined part, sound out smoothly, then read the word.

h<u>ea</u>d	<u>thr</u>ead	<u>d</u>ead	<u>r</u>ead	<u>br</u>ead

3. **ACCURACY/FLUENCY BUILDING** For each column, have students say any underlined part, then read each word. Next, have them read the column.

A1 Mixed Practice	B1 Related Words	C1 Multisyllabic Words	D1 Word Endings	E1 Tricky Words
<u>ce</u>lls	health	crea•tures	slime	blood
f<u>oo</u>l	healthy	de•com•pos•er	slimy	hearts
<u>shr</u>ed	healthier	tal•ent		breaks
s<u>oi</u>l		pro•vides	simple	wormy
s<u>ea</u>l	educate		simply	answer
gr<u>ow</u>	educated	creatures		
p<u>u</u>mp	education	decomposer	**D2** Rhyming Words	
<u>ch</u>ange		talent	hung	
b<u>a</u>sed		provides	sung	
fl<u>o</u>ss			lung	

4. **WORDS IN CONTEXT** Have students use the sounds and word parts they know to figure out the word. Then have students read the sentence.

A	di•gest	Earthworms eat and <u>digest</u> decaying plants and animals.
B	ru•in	We planned a special picnic. I hope the rain doesn't <u>ruin</u> our day.
C	false	Something that is not true is <u>false</u>.
D	se•cret	I can't tell you. It's a <u>secret</u>.

5. **MORPHOGRAPHS AND AFFIXES** Have students read each underlined part, then the word.

<u>re</u>cycle	<u>section</u>	<u>between</u>	enorm<u>ous</u>	activit<u>y</u>

6. **GENERALIZATION** Have students read the paragraph silently, then out loud. (New words: stuffy, waste)

My sister and I do not like catching colds. Our noses get stuffy, and it is hard to breathe. Our bodies feel tired, and all we do is sleep all day. We cannot do anything special. What a waste of time! It is much better to be healthy!

MAIN IDEA AND SUPPORTING DETAILS

FOCUS LESSON Skills and Strategies

PURPOSE

This lesson provides explicit instruction in identifying the topic of a paragraph, selecting interesting or important details, and constructing a main idea. The lesson prepares students for Comprehension and Skill Work.

COMPREHENSION PROCESSES

Understand, Analyze

PROCEDURES

PREP NOTE

To demonstrate how to complete the exercise, use an overhead of the page in the students' *Exercise Book 3*, write on a transparency placed over the page, or use a paper copy.

① INTRODUCTION

Introduce the main idea and supporting details. Say something like:

A main idea tells us the most important thing about a topic.

Today, we're going to work on a strategy for figuring out the main idea of a longer paragraph.

② MAIN IDEA AND SUPPORTING DETAILS

Identifying—Topic, Facts/Details; Using Graphic Organizer; Drawing Conclusions; Summarizing—Main Idea

• Have students read the paragraph and identify the topic.

Read the paragraph in the gray box. (What are the most important . . .)

Read Item 2. (What is the topic of the paragraph?)

What should I write for the topic? (krill)

• Demonstrate identifying an important fact. Have a student model. Then have students identify other important facts with their partner.

Let's think about the different facts we learned about krill.

I learned that krill are small shrimp-like animals.

[Marsha], what did you learn? (Krill are eaten by fish, birds, and whales.)

Excellent. Everyone, tell your partner another important fact about krill.

• Have students identify three details to write in the graphic organizer. Write the details in the graphic organizer. Have students read the phrases written.

• Guide students in writing a main idea statement.

What's our topic? (krill) What is the most important thing our facts tell us about krill? (Krill are important to many animals. Krill are important in the food chain. Krill are important in the ocean food chain . . .)

Those are all great ways to state the main idea.

• Write a main idea statement on the graphic organizer.

③ MAKE THE STEPS IN THE MAIN IDEA STRATEGY EXPLICIT

Have students discuss the main idea strategy by reading the statements in the box and reviewing the steps they completed.

Science Digest

Unit 17 Exercise 3b (Focus Lesson)

Use after Exercise 3a and before 10 Great Reasons to Be an Earthworm and
More About the 10 Great Reasons to Be an Earthworm

FOCUS LESSON Skills and Strategies

Main Idea and Supporting Details

1 **Read the following paragraph.**

What are the most important animals in the ocean food chain?
Krill! Krill are small shrimp-like animals that live in the ocean.
They eat tiny ocean plants that drift near the ocean's surface. Krill
are eaten by fish, birds, and whales. They are the main food for
hundreds of animals. Without krill, many animals would die.

STOP
Don't write
in your
Exercise
Book.

2 **What is the topic of the paragraph?** _krill_

(Accept any reasonable response.)

3 **List important details in the boxes.**

- _shrimp-like animals_ _____

- _eaten by fish, birds,_
  and whales

- _many animals would die_
  without krill

4 **Write a main idea.**

What do all of the
details tell you
about krill?

(Accept any reasonable response.)

Krill are very important
animals in the ocean
food chain.
_____

Main Idea Strategy

1. Read the paragraph.
2. Identify the topic.
3. Write important details.
4. Identify the most important thing
   the details tell you about the topic.
5. Write a main idea.

COMPREHENSION PROCESSES

Understand, Apply, Analyze

PROCEDURES

Introducing Vocabulary

> ☆ **floss** ☆ **decay**
> ☆ **decomposer** ☆ **digest**
> ☆ **recycle** ☆ **educated guess**

- For each vocabulary word, have students read the word by parts, then read the whole word.
- Read the student-friendly explanations to students as they follow with their fingers. Then have students use the vocabulary word by following the gray text.
- Review and discuss the photos and illustrations.

> USING VOCABULARY

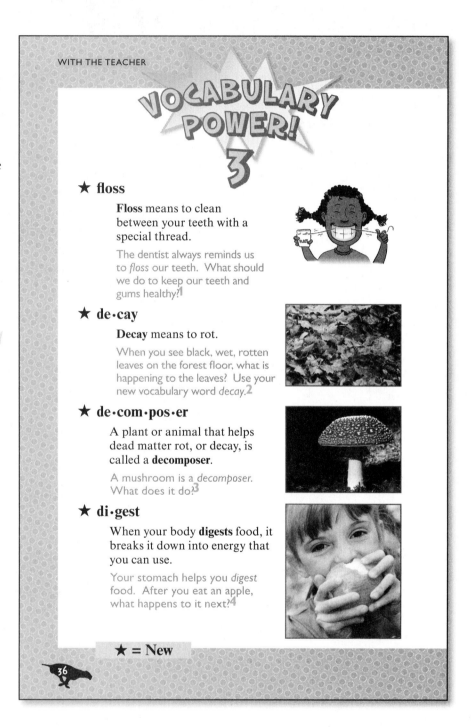

WITH THE TEACHER

VOCABULARY POWER! 3

★ floss

Floss means to clean between your teeth with a special thread.

The dentist always reminds us to *floss* our teeth. What should we do to keep our teeth and gums healthy?[1]

★ de·cay

Decay means to rot.

When you see black, wet, rotten leaves on the forest floor, what is happening to the leaves? Use your new vocabulary word *decay*.[2]

★ de·com·pos·er

A plant or animal that helps dead matter rot, or decay, is called a **decomposer**.

A mushroom is a *decomposer*. What does it do?[3]

★ di·gest

When your body **digests** food, it breaks it down into energy that you can use.

Your stomach helps you *digest* food. After you eat an apple, what happens to it next?[4]

★ = New

36

1 **Apply:** Inferring; Using Vocabulary—floss (We should floss our teeth.)

2 **Apply:** Explaining; Using Vocabulary—decay (The leaves are decaying.)

3 **Understand:** Explaining; Defining and Using Vocabulary—decomposer, decay (A mushroom helps dead things decay.)

4 **Understand:** Explaining; Using Vocabulary—digest (After you eat an apple, your body digests it.)

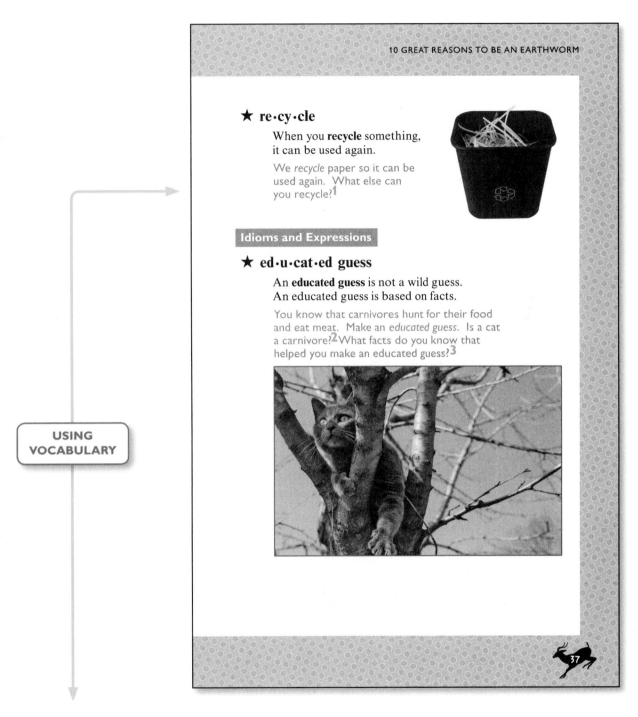

10 GREAT REASONS TO BE AN EARTHWORM

★ **re·cy·cle**

When you **recycle** something, it can be used again.

We *recycle* paper so it can be used again. What else can you recycle?[1]

Idioms and Expressions

★ **ed·u·cat·ed guess**

An **educated guess** is not a wild guess. An educated guess is based on facts.

You know that carnivores hunt for their food and eat meat. Make an *educated guess*. Is a cat a carnivore?[2] What facts do you know that helped you make an educated guess?[3]

USING VOCABULARY

37

[1] **Apply:** Making Connections; Using Vocabulary—recycle (You can recycle glass, plastic, soda cans . . .)

[2] **Analyze:** Classifying (yes)

[3] **Analyze:** Inferring; **Apply:** Explaining; **Understand:** Using Idioms and Expressions—educated guess (A cat eats mice, birds, and fish. It eats mostly meat, so I think a cat is a carnivore.)

"10 GREAT REASONS TO BE AN EARTHWORM" INSTRUCTIONS

Students read "10 Great Reasons to Be an Earthworm" on pages 38–41 with the teacher. Students read "More About the 10 Great Reasons to Be an Earthworm" on pages 42–45 on their own.

COMPREHENSION PROCESSES

Remember, Understand, Apply, Evaluate

PROCEDURES

1. Reviewing "What's at the Top?"

Summarizing—Facts; Describing; Explaining; Using Vocabulary—food chain, herbivore, prey; Making Judgments

Discuss the questions from Setting a Purpose. Say something like:

Yesterday, you read the article "What's at the Top?" That was a fun article full of facts! Let's see what you learned.

What is at the top of the food chain? Describe the food chain. (The lion is the top of the food chain. The lion eats herbivores like zebras and giraffes. The herbivores eat grass.)

How does this animal hunt for its prey? (The lionesses work together to hunt for food. Some of the lionesses move into the open so the prey can see them. Other lionesses sneak up on an animal from behind.)

How do the baby animals learn to hunt? (The cubs play with each other to learn hunting skills. They watch their mother, and they learn from their mistakes.)

Do you think this animal is intelligent? Why or why not? (Yes, they're intelligent because they learn. They can trick other animals. They learn from their mistakes . . .)

2. Introducing "10 Great Reasons to Be an Earthworm"

Identifying—Title, Author, Topic/Main Idea

Discuss the title and author. Say something like:

We've been learning about the food chain. Today, we will read about a decomposer, an animal that helps dead plants and animals rot. You'll learn how decomposers help the food chain.

What's the title of this article? (10 Great Reasons to Be an Earthworm)

Find the author's name. Her last name is pronounced *Wah-tah-nah-bay.*

Who is the author? (Ann Watanabe) What is this article about? (earthworms)

What do you think the main idea of the article is? (It's great to be an earthworm . . .)

3. First Reading
  • Ask questions and discuss the text as indicated by the gray text.
    If students have difficulty comprehending, think aloud with them or reread the portion of the story that answers the question. Repeat the question.
  • Mix group and individual turns, independent of your voice.
  • After reading the story, practice any difficult words and reread, if appropriate.

4. Second Reading, Short Passage Practice: Developing Prosody
  • Demonstrate expressive, fluent reading of the first paragraph on page 40.
  • Guide practice with your voice.
  • Provide individual turns while others track with their fingers and whisper read.
  • Repeat with one paragraph or page at a time, as time allows.

10 GREAT REASONS TO BE AN EARTHWORM

by Ann Watanabe

1. Earthworms never need to take a bath.

2. Earthworms never need glasses.

3. Earthworms never get stuffy noses.

4. Earthworms have a lot of heart.

5. Earthworms can grow new tails when their tails get cut off.

38

FOCUS ON HUMOR, VIEWING

Before reading, say something like:
Ms. Watanabe and the artist had fun with this cartoon. All of the information is factual, but the pictures and facts will make you laugh. The first item says, "Earthworms never need to take a bath." That's a fact, but it's a silly fact. Whoever thought about earthworms taking baths? The author must have a good sense of humor.

Look at the picture. What did the artist do to make this a funny fact? (The worm is wearing a shower cap, and he's in a bathtub. He even has a scrub brush in his tail.)

After reading each item, have students discuss how the author's ideas and the cartoon work together for a little fun.

WITH THE TEACHER

The Most Important Reason
It's Great to Be an Earthworm

Earthworms take care of the Earth. They are an important part of the food chain. They eat decaying plants and animals. They are called decomposers. Decomposers change dead stuff into food for plants.

Earthworms use their mouths to pull the dead leaves, grass, seeds, or the remains of dead animals into tunnels in the ground. Earthworms shred the dead matter and then digest it.

**Worm
Waste**

**FOCUS ON
VOCABULARY—**
decomposer

**After completing the
page, say something like:**
Earthworms change dead
stuff into food for plants.
That means they are . . .
decomposers.

How does this help
take care of the Earth?
(Earthworms make food
for plants. That helps the
Earth. Earthworms get
rid of dead stuff.)

Finally, earthworms leave behind their waste. The waste provides food for plants. It makes the soil rich. Plants grow well in soil that has been tended by earthworms.

> **Finish these three facts:**
>
> Decomposers change dead stuff into . . .[1]
>
> Decomposers make the soil . . .[2]
>
> Decomposers help plants . . .[3]

**COMPREHENDING
AS YOU GO**

[1] **Remember:** Identifying—Fact (food for plants)
[2] **Remember:** Identifying—Fact (rich)
[3] **Remember:** Identifying—Fact (grow well)

10 GREAT REASONS TO BE AN EARTHWORM

Make an Educated Guess

What would happen if you planted seeds in two flowerpots, then added worms to the soil in the first pot, but not to the second? If you took care of both pots in the same way, which pot would have bigger, healthier plants?

FOCUS ON IDIOMS AND EXPRESSIONS— *educated guess*

After completing the page, say something like:

You just made an educated guess about which pot would have a bigger, healthier plant. What does *educated guess* mean? (It's a guess based on facts.)

Your educated guess was that the plant that had worms in its pot would be healthier. Use the facts you know to explain why. (The pot with the earthworms would be healthier because earthworms make the soil richer.)

That's exactly right. Your guess was based on what you know, so it was an . . . educated guess.

> **Wormy but true . . .**
>
> Decomposers recycle dead stuff. They turn the dead matter into food for plants.

41

"MORE ABOUT THE 10 GREAT REASONS TO BE AN EARTHWORM" INSTRUCTIONS

Students read "More About the 10 Great Reasons to Be an Earthworm" on pages 42–45 without the teacher, independently or with partners.

COMPREHENSION PROCESSES

Remember, Understand, Analyze, Evaluate

PROCEDURES FOR READING ON YOUR OWN

1. Getting Ready

Have students turn to page 42. Tell students they are going to read "More About the 10 Great Reasons to Be an Earthworm" on their own.

2. Setting a Purpose

Identifying—Title, Facts; Responding; Comparing/Contrasting

Establish a purpose for reading. Say something like:

What's the title of this article? (More About the 10 Great Reasons to Be an Earthworm)

We're going to find out more about those 10 reasons earthworms are great! As you read, think about how you would answer these questions:

- What are some reasons that it's great to be an earthworm?
- What do you think is the most interesting fact about earthworms?
- What can earthworms do that you can't do?

> **PREP NOTE**
> **Setting a Purpose**
> Write questions on a chalkboard, white board, or large piece of paper before working with your small group.

3. Reading on Your Own: Partner or Whisper Reading

- Have students take turns reading every other page with a partner or have students whisper read pages 42–45 on their own.
- Continue having students track each word with their fingers.

4. Comprehension and Skill Work

Tell students they will do Comprehension and Skill Activities 5 and 6 after they read on their own. Guide practice, as needed. For teacher directions, see pages 76 and 77.

5. Homework 3: Repeated Reading

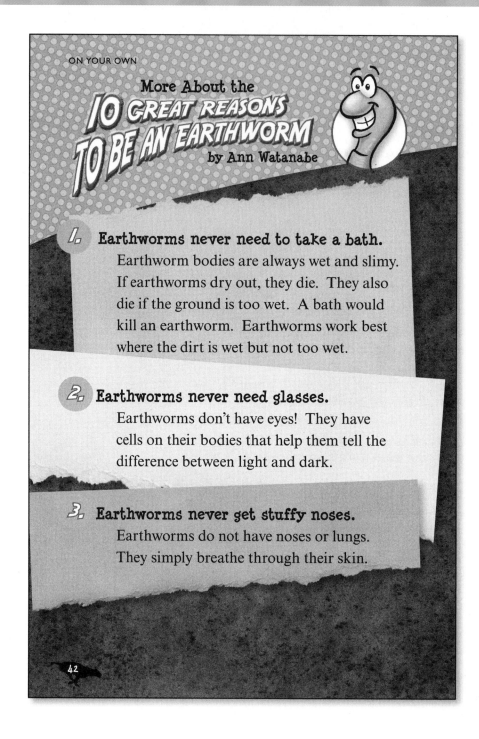

More About the
10 GREAT REASONS TO BE AN EARTHWORM
by Ann Watanabe

1. Earthworms never need to take a bath.

Earthworm bodies are always wet and slimy. If earthworms dry out, they die. They also die if the ground is too wet. A bath would kill an earthworm. Earthworms work best where the dirt is wet but not too wet.

2. Earthworms never need glasses.

Earthworms don't have eyes! They have cells on their bodies that help them tell the difference between light and dark.

3. Earthworms never get stuffy noses.

Earthworms do not have noses or lungs. They simply breathe through their skin.

42

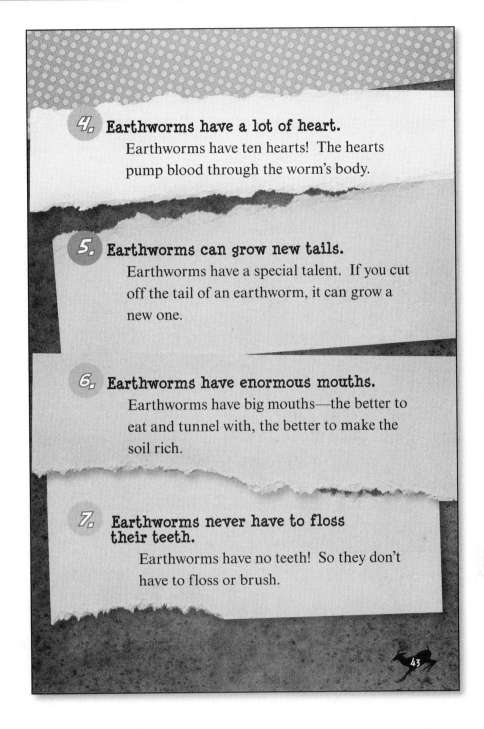

4. **Earthworms have a lot of heart.**

Earthworms have ten hearts! The hearts pump blood through the worm's body.

5. **Earthworms can grow new tails.**

Earthworms have a special talent. If you cut off the tail of an earthworm, it can grow a new one.

6. **Earthworms have enormous mouths.**

Earthworms have big mouths—the better to eat and tunnel with, the better to make the soil rich.

7. **Earthworms never have to floss their teeth.**

Earthworms have no teeth! So they don't have to floss or brush.

43

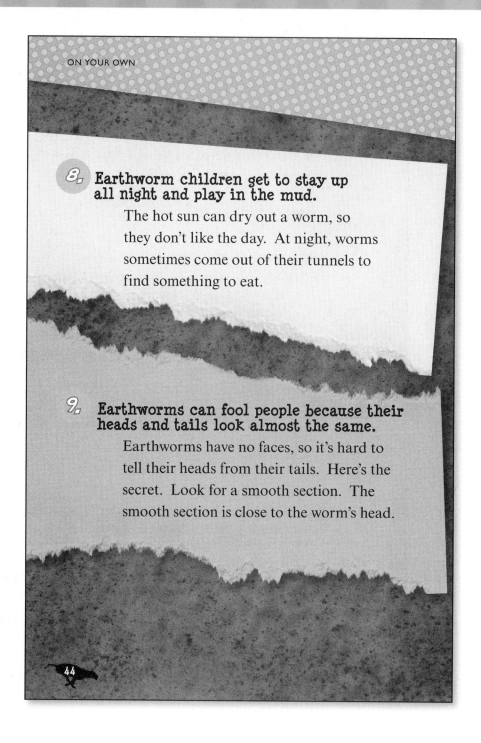

8. **Earthworm children get to stay up all night and play in the mud.**

The hot sun can dry out a worm, so they don't like the day. At night, worms sometimes come out of their tunnels to find something to eat.

9. **Earthworms can fool people because their heads and tails look almost the same.**

Earthworms have no faces, so it's hard to tell their heads from their tails. Here's the secret. Look for a smooth section. The smooth section is close to the worm's head.

44

MORE ABOUT THE 10 GREAT REASONS . . .

10. **Earthworms take care of the Earth.**
Earthworms are simple creatures, but they have been on Earth for about 300 million years—even before the dinosaurs. Worms keep our plants healthy. They help keep Earth green.

Quiz

True or False

1. Earthworms are great swimmers.
   T   F

2. Earthworms have big mouths but no teeth.
   T   F

3. Earthworms will ruin your garden!
   T   F

4. Earthworms love the hot sun.
   T   F

45

① **Understand:** Inferring—Fact; Test Taking (false)
② **Understand:** Identifying—Fact; Test Taking (true)
③ **Understand:** Inferring—Fact; Test Taking (false)
④ **Understand:** Identifying—Fact; Test Taking (false)

MAIN IDEA AND SUPPORTING DETAILS

COMPREHENSION PROCESSES

Remember, Understand, Apply, Analyze

WRITING TRAITS

Conventions—Complete Sentence, Capital, Period

Identifying—Topic

Using Graphic Organizer
Identifying—Supporting Details
Inferring—Main Idea
Drawing Conclusions
Sentence Writing

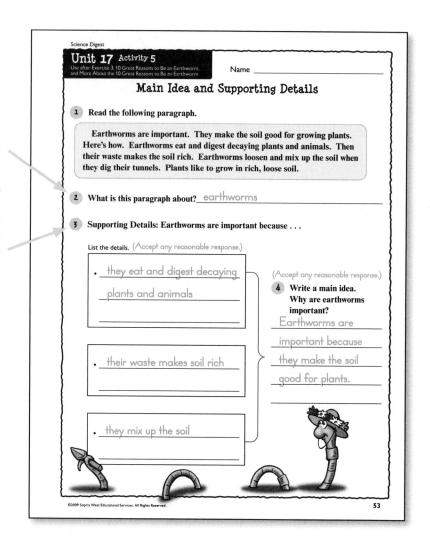

Science Digest

Unit 17 Activity 5
Use after Exercise 3, 10 Great Reasons to Be an Earthworm,
and More About the 10 Great Reasons to Be an Earthworm

Name _____

Main Idea and Supporting Details

1 Read the following paragraph.

> Earthworms are important. They make the soil good for growing plants. Here's how. Earthworms eat and digest decaying plants and animals. Then their waste makes the soil rich. Earthworms loosen and mix up the soil when they dig their tunnels. Plants like to grow in rich, loose soil.

2 What is this paragraph about? __earthworms__

3 Supporting Details: Earthworms are important because . . .

List the details. (Accept any reasonable response.)

- they eat and digest decaying plants and animals

- their waste makes soil rich

- they mix up the soil

(Accept any reasonable response.)

4 Write a main idea. Why are earthworms important?
Earthworms are important because they make the soil good for plants.

©2009 Sopris West Educational Services. All Rights Reserved.   53

PROCEDURES

For each step, demonstrate and guide practice, as needed. Then have students complete the page independently.

1. Topic: Answering Questions—Basic Instructions (Items 1, 2)
- Have students read the paragraph in the box.
- Have students read the question and write the topic in the blank.

2. Main Idea/Supporting Details: Hierarchy Chart—Specific Instructions (Item 3)
- Have students read the sentence stem, "Earthworms are important because . . . "
Then have students fill in each box with a supporting detail from the paragraph.
- Have students write the main idea sentence. Remind them to use a capital and a period.
Note: The main idea can be stated in a variety of ways.

★ = New in this unit

VOCABULARY AND ALPHABETICAL ORDER

COMPREHENSION PROCESSES

Understand, Apply

WRITING TRAITS

Conventions—Complete Sentence, Capital, Period

Alphabetical Order

Defining and Using Vocabulary— recycle; Illustrating

Defining and Using Vocabulary— predator; Illustrating

Defining and Using Vocabulary— nomadic; Illustrating

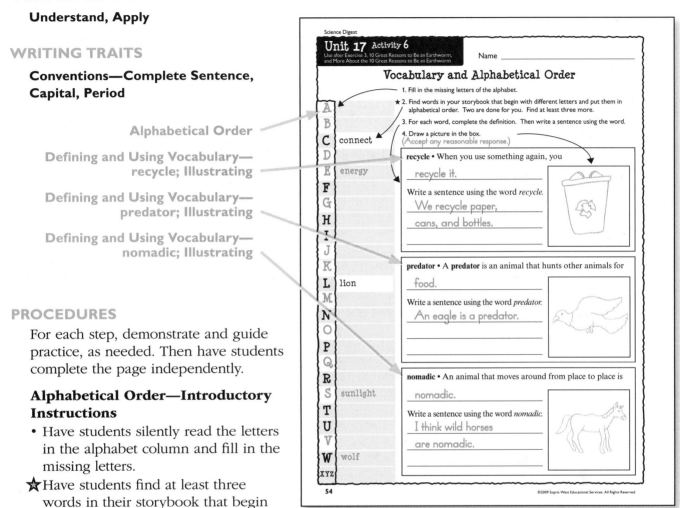

PROCEDURES

For each step, demonstrate and guide practice, as needed. Then have students complete the page independently.

Alphabetical Order—Introductory Instructions

• Have students silently read the letters in the alphabet column and fill in the missing letters.

★Have students find at least three words in their storybook that begin with different letters.

Write the words after the matching letter in the first column. Say something like:

You are going to find three words in your storybook that begin with different letters.

Then you'll write each word next to the letter it begins with. Two words are done for you.

Read the first word in the column. (connect)

Connect begins with the letter c, so it is written next to the letter c.

Read the next word. (lion) What letter is *lion* next to? (l)

Look in your storybook for a word that you would like to write.

[Jes], what word did you find? (herbivores) *Herbivores* is a great snazzy word.

Where will you write the word *herbivores*? (next to the letter h)

Find at least two more words from your storybook and write them next to the correct letters.

Vocabulary: Sentence Completion/Writing, Illustrating—Basic Instructions

• Have students read each vocabulary word and complete the sentence to define the word.

• Have students write a complete sentence using each word. Remind them to use a capital and a period.

• Have students draw a picture of the word or their sentence.

Self-monitoring

Have students check and correct their work.

❶ SOUND REVIEW
Use selected Sound Cards from Units 1–17.

❷ ACCURACY AND FLUENCY BUILDING
- For each task, have students say any underlined part, then read the word.
- Set a pace. Then have students read the whole words in each task and column.
- Provide repeated practice, building accuracy first, then fluency.

D1. Multisyllabic Words
- For the list of words divided by syllables, have students read each syllable, then the whole word. Use the word in a sentence, as appropriate.
- For the list of whole words, build accuracy and then fluency.

decomposer	The worm is a . . . *decomposer.*
intelligent	The rocket scientist was . . . *intelligent.*
predator	A lion is a . . . *predator.*
annelids	Some types of worms with segmented bodies are called . . . *annelids.*

E1. Tricky Words
- For each Tricky Word, have students use the sounds and word parts they know to silently sound out the word. Use the word in a sentence to help with pronunciation.
- If the word is unfamiliar, tell students the word.

nutrients

Look at the first word. Say the word parts with me. nu-tri-ents
Vitamins are *nutrients.* Animals and plants need nutrients to live and grow.
Use the word in this sentence. Animals and plants need . . . *nutrients.*
Read the word five times. (nutrients, nutrients, nutrients, nutrients, nutrients)

haiku

Look at the next word. The word is *haiku.* A haiku is a kind of Japanese poem.
Say the word. (haiku) A kind of Japanese poem is a . . . *haiku.*

truth	Honest Abe did not lie. He always told the . . . *truth.*
busy	Edward called his friend, but her phone was . . . *busy.*
prey	The lions hunted for . . . *prey.*
shovels	The workers dug holes with . . . *shovels.*

❸ NAMES AND PLACES

❹ MORPHOGRAPHS AND AFFIXES
⭐In Row A, introduce and practice the affix *-sion* and the related words.
  Your new affix is another spelling for /shun/. What does s-i-o-n say? (shun)
  Read each underlined part and then the whole word. (sion, discussion . . .)
- In Row B, have students read each affix and then the whole word.

❺ GENERALIZATION: READING NEW WORDS IN PARAGRAPHS
- Have students read the paragraph silently, then out loud. Tell students to use the sounds and word parts they know to read any difficult words.
- Repeat practice, as needed.

Science Digest

Unit 17 Exercise 4

Use before Digging Up the Truth, Garden Haiku, and
The Garden We Share, Chapter 1

1. SOUND REVIEW Use selected Sound Cards from Units 1–17.

2. ACCURACY/FLUENCY BUILDING For each column, have students say any underlined part, then read each word. Next, have them read the column.

A1 Mixed Practice	B1 Related Words	C1 Word Endings	D1 Multisyllabic Words	E1 Tricky Words
dr<u>ow</u>n	energy	thrive	de·com·pos·er	nutrients
K<u>nigh</u>t	energize	thriving	in·tel·li·gent	haiku
s<u>oi</u>l	energizing		pred·a·tor	truth
<u>kn</u>ocked	**B2** Word Endings	share	an·ne·lids	busy
dec<u>ay</u>		sharing		prey
b<u>ai</u>t	<u>seedlings</u>		decomposer	shovels
Billy	<u>squirming</u>	scurry	intelligent	
Ty	<u>sprouting</u>	scurried	predator	
<u>Au</u>stin	<u>tunneling</u>		annelids	
	<u>sincerely</u>			

3. NAMES AND PLACES Have students use the sounds they know to figure out the words.

Oregon	Hawaii	Hilo	Josephine	Dylan	Albany

4. MORPHOGRAPHS AND AFFIXES Have students practice reading "-sion" and the related words. For Row B, have students read the underlined part, then the word.

A	★ -sion	discus<u>sion</u>	mis<u>sion</u>	permis<u>sion</u>
B	vib<u>ra</u>tion	scientif<u>ic</u>	communit<u>y</u>	exceptio<u>n</u>ally

5. GENERALIZATION Have students read the paragraph silently, then out loud. (New words: Nate, Michael, vacant, cabbage, lettuce, paper)

Nate and Michael decided to make a garden in the vacant lot. They worked very hard. Now they have a thriving garden. There are bees buzzing around the sweet flowers. The cabbage, lettuce, and tomatoes are growing in the warm sunlight. Soon they will have a garden full of food to share. Someone from the local paper even came to take a picture of the garden.

COMPREHENSION PROCESSES

Understand, Apply

PROCEDURES

1. Introducing Vocabulary

> decomposer, energy
> ★vacant ★scurry
> ★thrive ★thriving,
> community, predator, prey

- For each vocabulary word, have students read the word by parts, then read the whole word.
- Read the student-friendly explanations to students as they follow with their fingers. Then have students use the vocabulary word by following the gray text.
- Review and discuss the photos and illustrations.

USING VOCABULARY

WITH THE TEACHER

VOCABULARY POWER! 4

de·com·pos·er

A plant or animal that helps dead matter rot, or decay, is called a **decomposer**.

An earthworm is a decomposer. What does it do? [1]

en·er·gy

Energy is the power to do things.

What gives plants the energy to grow? [2]

★ va·cant

Vacant means empty. A building, a room, or even a chair can be vacant.

No one was living in the house. The house was vacant. Describe the house in the picture. [3]

★ scur·ry

Scurry means to move quickly with small steps.

The little mouse scurried into its hole. Show me how you might scurry across the room. [4]

★ = New

46

① **Understand:** Defining and/or Using Vocabulary—decomposer, decay (An earthworm helps dead matter decay.)

② **Understand:** Explaining; Using Vocabulary—energy (The sun gives plants energy to grow.)

③ **Understand:** Describing; Using Vocabulary—vacant (The house is vacant.)

④ **Apply:** Demonstrating; **Understand:** Defining Vocabulary—scurry

★ = New in this unit

2. Now You Try It!

- Read or paraphrase the directions.
- Then, for each word, have students read the word by parts, then read the whole word.
- Have students explain or define the word in their own words. Say something like:

  Look at the first word. Say the parts, then read the whole word.

  (com•mu•ni•ty, community) Now, let's pretend that we're going to explain or define the word *community* to a friend. [Jamal], what would you say?

  Start with "A *community* is . . ." (A community is people living and working together.)

  That's right. Our neighborhood is a community. It's full of people living and working together.

- Have students turn to the appropriate page in the glossary and discuss how their definitions are the same as or different from the glossary's. Your students may like their definitions better.

Note: By defining a word in their own words, students are demonstrating depth of word knowledge. Verbatim responses only demonstrate memorization. Encourage paraphrasing.

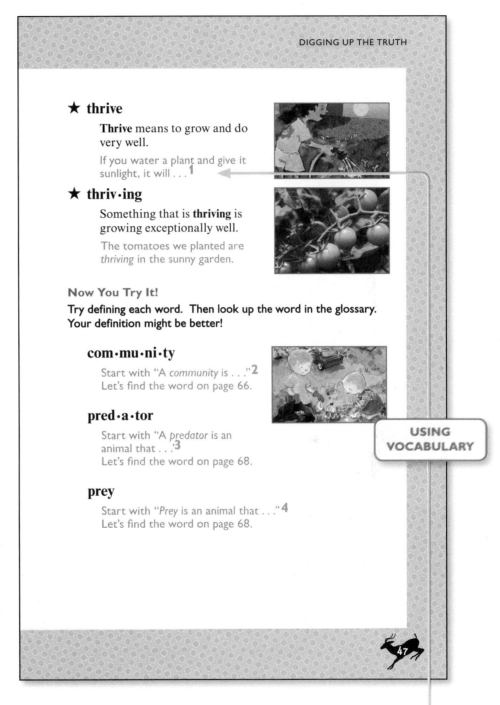

DIGGING UP THE TRUTH

★ **thrive**

Thrive means to grow and do very well.

If you water a plant and give it sunlight, it will . . .**1**

★ **thriv·ing**

Something that is **thriving** is growing exceptionally well.

The tomatoes we planted are *thriving* in the sunny garden.

Now You Try It!

Try defining each word. Then look up the word in the glossary. Your definition might be better!

com·mu·ni·ty

Start with "A *community* is . . ."**2**
Let's find the word on page 66.

pred·a·tor

Start with "A *predator* is an animal that . . ."**3**
Let's find the word on page 68.

prey

Start with "*Prey* is an animal that . . ."**4**
Let's find the word on page 68.

USING VOCABULARY

47

❶ **Apply:** Using Vocabulary—thrive (thrive)

❷ **Understand:** Defining and Using Vocabulary—community; Using Glossary (A community is people or animals that live and work together . . .)

❸ **Understand:** Defining and Using Vocabulary—predator; Using Glossary (A predator is an animal that hunts and eats other animals.)

❹ **Understand:** Defining and Using Vocabulary—prey; Using Glossary (Prey is an animal that is hunted. A rabbit might be the prey of an owl . . .)

"DIGGING UP THE TRUTH" INSTRUCTIONS

Students read "Digging Up the Truth" on pages 48–50 and "Garden Haiku" on page 51 with the teacher. Students read Chapter 1 of "The Garden We Share" on their own during their independent work.

COMPREHENSION PROCESSES

Remember, Understand, Apply, Analyze, Evaluate

PROCEDURES

1. **Reviewing "More About the 10 Great Reasons to Be an Earthworm"**

   Identifying—Facts; Responding; Comparing/Contrasting

   Discuss the questions from Setting a Purpose. Say something like:

   Yesterday, you learned even more about earthworms.

   What are some reasons it's great to be an earthworm? (Earthworms have no teeth so they do not have to brush their teeth. Earthworms never get stuffy noses. Earthworms get to stay up all night and play in the mud . . .)

   What do you think is the most interesting fact about earthworms? (I think the most interesting fact is . . .)

   What can earthworms do that you can't do? (Earthworms can grow a new tail. Earthworms can fool people because their heads and tails look almost the same . . .)

2. **Introducing "Digging Up the Truth"**

   Identifying—Title, Author

   Discuss what "Letters to the Editor" are. Say something like:

   We're going to read "Letters to the Editor."

   Remember that the editor of a magazine is in charge of everything that goes in the magazine. You can write to the editor of a magazine to share your thoughts or ask questions. What's the title of this part? (Digging Up the Truth)

   Who is the editor answering the letters? (Professor Worm)

3. **First Reading**
   • Ask questions and discuss the letters and responses as indicated in the teacher's guide.
   • Mix group and individual turns, independent of your voice. Have students work toward a group accuracy goal of 0–2 errors. Quietly keep track of errors made by all students in the group.
   • After reading the letters and responses, practice any difficult words. Reread the story if students have not reached the accuracy goal.

4. **Second Reading, Short Passage Practice: Developing Prosody**
   • Demonstrate expressive, fluent reading of a letter and its reply.
   • Guide practice with your voice.
   • Provide individual turns while others track with their fingers and whisper read.
   • Repeat with another selected letter and reply.

WITH THE TEACHER

Digging Up the Truth

With Professor Worm

Ask Professor Worm your science questions!

Dear Professor Worm,

My brother Dylan and I had a long discussion about you. We have lots of **questions. Are earthworms insects? Can you see in the dark? Can you swim?**

PROFESSOR WORM

Ty and Dylan
Hilo, Hawaii

Dear Ty and Dylan,

What excellent questions! Earthworms are not insects! If you want to be scientific, we are annelids. Earthworms cannot see, but we can feel vibrations and sense light. That is how we get around in dark tunnels.

We cannot swim. We would drown if we were even in a puddle. If our tunnels get filled with rainwater, we have to leave.

Sincerely,
Professor Worm

48

PRIMING BACKGROUND KNOWLEDGE

After reading Ty and Dylan's letter, say something like:

The kids want to know if earthworms are insects. What do you remember about insects?
(They have six legs and three body parts.)
Do you think earthworms are insects? Why or why not?
(Worms don't have legs and three body parts.)

I think you're right. Do you remember what kind of animal a worm is?

Let's see what Professor Worm says.

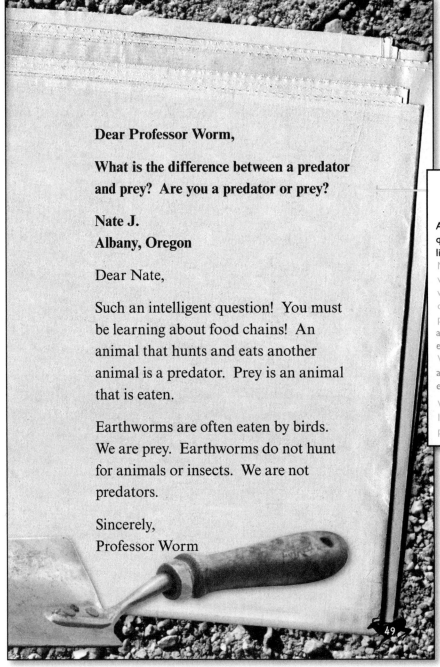

Dear Professor Worm,

What is the difference between a predator and prey? Are you a predator or prey?

Nate J.
Albany, Oregon

Dear Nate,

Such an intelligent question! You must be learning about food chains! An animal that hunts and eats another animal is a predator. Prey is an animal that is eaten.

Earthworms are often eaten by birds. We are prey. Earthworms do not hunt for animals or insects. We are not predators.

Sincerely,
Professor Worm

49

FOCUS ON VOCABULARY—
predator, prey

After reading Nate's question, say something like:

Nate knows some snazzy vocabulary words. How would you answer his question, "What is a predator?" (A predator is an animal that hunts and eats other animals.)
What is prey? (Prey is the animal that is hunted and eaten.)

What do you think?
Is Professor Worm a predator or prey?

WITH THE TEACHER

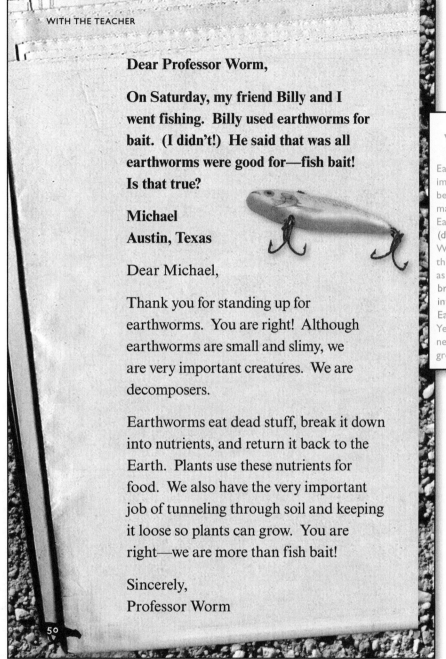

Dear Professor Worm,

On Saturday, my friend Billy and I went fishing. Billy used earthworms for bait. (I didn't!) He said that was all earthworms were good for—fish bait! Is that true?

**Michael
Austin, Texas**

Dear Michael,

Thank you for standing up for earthworms. You are right! Although earthworms are small and slimy, we are very important creatures. We are decomposers.

Earthworms eat dead stuff, break it down into nutrients, and return it back to the Earth. Plants use these nutrients for food. We also have the very important job of tunneling through soil and keeping it loose so plants can grow. You are right—we are more than fish bait!

Sincerely,
Professor Worm

50

FOCUS ON VOCABULARY— decomposer

Earthworms are important to the Earth because they help dead matter rot, or decay. Earthworms are . . . (decomposers).
What other important things do earthworms do as decomposers? (They break down dead matter into nutrients for the Earth.)
Yes, animals and plants need nutrients to live and grow.

WITH THE TEACHER

GARDEN HAIKU

Planting, rain waters

Warm energizing sunlight

Sharing and working

Slimy worms squirming

Bees buzzing, seedlings sprouting

A thriving garden

Colorful flowers

Lettuce, green beans, cabbage, peas

A garden we share

—Ann Watanabe

FOCUS ON POETRY—HAIKU

Before reading the poem, say something like:

A *haiku* is a type of poem from Japan. Each poem has three lines.

Look at "Garden Haiku." There are actually three haiku. How many lines does each haiku have? (three)
The first line has five syllables. Read the first line and count the syllables. (Planting, rain waters)
How many syllables? (five)

Read the next line and count the syllables. (Warm, energizing sunlight)
How many syllables? (seven) Yes, seven. The second line in each haiku has seven syllables.

Read the last line. It has five syllables. Read and count the syllables. (Sharing and working)

Let's read the whole verse. (Planting, rain waters; Warm energizing sunlight; Sharing and working)

51

Note: These poems introduce the next story, "The Garden We Share," a fictional narrative about a community garden.

CHAPTER 1 INSTRUCTIONS

Students read pages 53–55 without the teacher, independently or with partners.

COMPREHENSION PROCESSES

Remember, Understand, Apply

PROCEDURES FOR READING ON YOUR OWN

1. Getting Ready

Have students turn to Chapter 1 of "The Garden We Share" on page 53.

2. Setting a Purpose

Identifying—Title, Narrator, Problem, Goal

Establish a purpose for reading. Say something like:

Sometimes magazines also have fictional stories in them.

The next story we read will be fictional.

What's the title of the story? (The Garden We Share)

Let's read to find out the answers to these questions:

- Who is telling the story?
- What is the problem?
- What did the main character want? What was her goal?

> **PREP NOTE**
>
> **Setting a Purpose**
>
> Write questions on a chalkboard, white board, or large piece of paper before working with your small group.

3. Reading on Your Own: Partner or Whisper Reading

- Have students take turns reading every other page with a partner or have students whisper read pages 53–55 on their own.
- Continue having students track each word with their fingers.
- Have students ask themselves or their partners the gray text questions.

4. Comprehension and Skill Work

Tell students that they will do Comprehension and Skill Activities 7 and 8 after they read on their own. Guide practice, as needed. For teacher directions, see pages 92 and 93.

5. Homework 4: Repeated Reading

ON YOUR OWN

The Garden We Share

by Myka-Lynne Sokoloff

illustrated by Tatjana Mai-Wyss

52

THE GARDEN WE SHARE

Chapter 1
A Perfect Place

Mama looked out the window and sighed. "That vacant lot is such a mess. Every time I look at it, it makes me sad," she said.

"Why don't we clean it up?" I asked.

"Oh, Cara. It's just too much work for the two of us," she said.

I was quiet, but my brain was busy. I came up with a splendid idea. "Mama, may I go to Josephine's?" I asked.

With Mama's permission, I scurried to my best friend's home and knocked on the door. I told Josephine my idea. "Cool!" she said.

~What do you think Cara's splendid idea is?1

53

COMPREHENDING AS YOU GO

❶ **Apply:** Predicting (She will get her friend Josephine to help clean up the lot . . .)

ON YOUR OWN

I knew I could count on Josephine. We were so excited!

Josephine and I went up and down the block knocking on doors and ringing doorbells. We took turns telling the neighbors about our idea. They all thought it was an awesome plan!

The next Saturday, all the neighbors came out to help. I was impressed! Some had empty bags for trash. Other people carried rakes and shovels. Everyone got busy cleaning up the lot. We picked up empty bottles and scraps of paper. Then we raked the dirt so it was nice and smooth. The whole street looked so much better when we finished.

"It's so sunny here," said Mr. Phillips.

"This lot would be a great spot for growing tomatoes," said Mrs. Knight.

Why is the lot a great spot for growing tomatoes?1
What else does a plant need to grow?2

54

COMPREHENDING
AS YOU GO

❶ **Understand:** Explaining (The lot is a great spot to grow tomatoes because it's so sunny.)

❷ **Apply:** Explaining (Besides sunlight, plants need air and water to grow . . .)

THE GARDEN WE SHARE

We all agreed the lot would make a perfect place for a garden. Everyone said they would help.

Mr. Phillips said, "I have a hose."

"I have some seeds," said Mama.

"I have some extra tomato plants," added Mrs. Knight.

"This will be perfect," I thought.

55

ASKING QUESTIONS • LETTER WRITING

COMPREHENSION PROCESSES

Apply, Create

WRITING TRAITS

**Ideas and Content
Conventions—Complete Sentence,
Capital, Period, Question Mark
Presentation**

Asking Questions; Generating Ideas
Using Vocabulary—food chain
Sentence Writing

Asking Questions; Generating Ideas
Using Vocabulary—food chain,
herbivore, carnivore, decomposer
Paragraph Writing

PROCEDURES

For each step, demonstrate and
guide practice, as needed. Then
have students complete the page
independently.

1. **Question Writing—Specific
   Instructions** (Item 1)

   Have students read the directions,
   then write at least two questions.
   Say something like:

   You're going to write a pretend letter to Professor Worm. First, think about questions you
   might want to ask about earthworms or other animals in the food chain. (How fast can zebras
   run? How long have earthworms been on Earth? What are earthworms' favorite foods . . .)
   You can write two of those questions for Item 1 or write your own questions.

2. **Letter Writing—Specific Instructions** (Item 2)

   • Have students read the directions, then write a letter to Professor Worm. Remind them
     they can use the questions they already wrote. Say something like:

     Read the directions for Item 2. (Write a letter to Professor Worm. Introduce yourself . . .)
     Look at the letter in the box. What is the first thing that you will write? (the date)
     Yes. The letter already starts with . . . (Dear Professor Worm).
     If I were writing a letter, I could say: "I am a teacher at [Emily Dickinson School]. My class is
     learning about zebras. This is my question: How fast can zebras run?"
     The letter has a closing for me. It says "Sincerely," so I can sign my name on the bottom.

   • Guide students as they discuss ideas to be included in their own letters.

   • Remind students to begin their sentences with a capital and end with a period or a
     question mark.

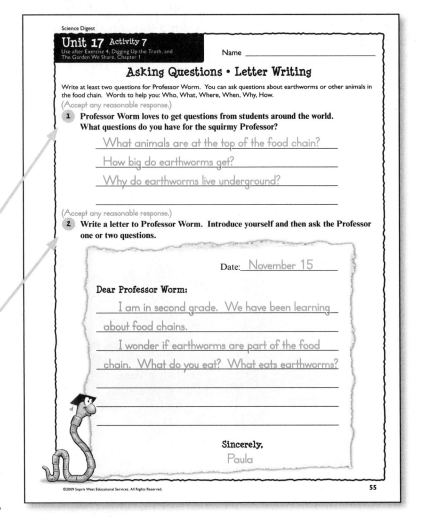

Science Digest

Unit 17 Activity 7
Use after Exercise 4, Digging Up the Truth, and
The Garden We Share, Chapter 1

Name _____

Asking Questions • Letter Writing

Write at least two questions for Professor Worm. You can ask questions about earthworms or other animals in
the food chain. Words to help you: Who, What, Where, When, Why, How.
(Accept any reasonable response.)

1 Professor Worm loves to get questions from students around the world.
   What questions do you have for the squirmy Professor?

   What animals are at the top of the food chain?
   How big do earthworms get?
   Why do earthworms live underground?

(Accept any reasonable response.)

2 Write a letter to Professor Worm. Introduce yourself and then ask the Professor
   one or two questions.

   Date: November 15

   Dear Professor Worm:

   I am in second grade. We have been learning
   about food chains.
   I wonder if earthworms are part of the food
   chain. What do you eat? What eats earthworms?

   Sincerely,
   Paula

©2009 Sopris West Educational Services. All Rights Reserved.   55

PASSAGE READING FLUENCY

FLUENCY

Accuracy, Expression, Rate

PROCEDURES

For each step, demonstrate and guide practice, as needed. Then have students complete the page independently.

Passage Reading—Basic Instructions

- Have students read the practice words first.
- Have students finger track and whisper read the story two times—the first time for accuracy and the second for expression.
  Have students cross out the chain links each time they finish the passage.
- Have students do a one-minute Timed Reading and cross out the timer.

> **ACCURACY PRECEDES RATE**
> **(Reminder)**
> Students should read the story with a high degree of accuracy before proceeding to Timed Readings. Reading for increased rate before establishing a high degree of accuracy may encourage students to guess at words.

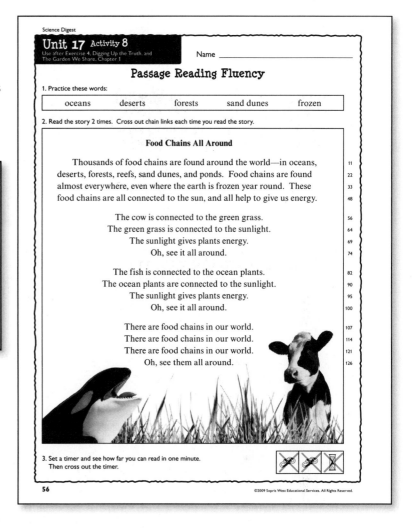

Science Digest

Unit 17 Activity 8
Use after Exercise 4, Digging Up the Truth, and The Garden We Share, Chapter 1

Name _____

Passage Reading Fluency

1. Practice these words:

| oceans | deserts | forests | sand dunes | frozen |

2. Read the story 2 times. Cross out chain links each time you read the story.

Food Chains All Around

Thousands of food chains are found around the world—in oceans, deserts, forests, reefs, sand dunes, and ponds. Food chains are found almost everywhere, even where the earth is frozen year round. These food chains are all connected to the sun, and all help to give us energy.

The cow is connected to the green grass.
The green grass is connected to the sunlight.
The sunlight gives plants energy.
Oh, see it all around.

The fish is connected to the ocean plants.
The ocean plants are connected to the sunlight.
The sunlight gives plants energy.
Oh, see it all around.

There are food chains in our world.
There are food chains in our world.
There are food chains in our world.
Oh, see them all around.

11
22
33
48
56
64
69
74
82
90
95
100
107
114
121
126

3. Set a timer and see how far you can read in one minute. Then cross out the timer.

56

©2009 Sopris West Educational Services. All Rights Reserved.

1 SOUND REVIEW

2 SOUND PRACTICE
- For each task, have students spell and say the focus sound in the gray bar. For the Bossy E, read the header.
- Next, have students read each underlined sound, the word, then the whole column.
- Repeat with each column, building accuracy first, then fluency.

3 ACCURACY AND FLUENCY BUILDING
- For each task, have students say any underlined part, then read the word.
- Set a pace. Then have students read the whole words in each task and column.
- Provide repeated practice, building accuracy first, then fluency.

D1. Multisyllabic Words
- For the list of words divided by syllables, have students read each syllable, then the whole word. Use the words in sentences, as appropriate.
- For the list of whole words, build accuracy and then fluency.

handles	Byron crashed his bike when he lost his grip on the . . . *handles*.
ribbons	Tied at the bottom of the girl's braids were pretty . . . *ribbons*.
continued	The TV show was to be . . . *continued*.

E1. Tricky Words
- For each Tricky Word, have students use the sounds and word parts they know to silently sound out the word. Use the word in a sentence to help with pronunciation.

aphid
Look at the first word. This word is just a little bit tricky. The first sound is /āāā/.
Read the word. (aphid) An *aphid* is a kind of insect that eats plants.
Read the word three times. (aphid, aphid, aphid)

nectar
Look at the next word. Say the word parts with me. nec-tar
Nectar is a sweet liquid found in flowers. A sweet liquid found in flowers is called . . . *nectar*.
Read the word three times. (nectar, nectar, nectar)

pulling	The oxen's job was . . . *pulling* . . . the cart.
piece	She cut the apple into slices and gave everyone a . . . *piece*.

- Have students go back and read the whole words in the column.

4 WORDS IN CONTEXT
For each word, have students use the sounds and word parts they know to silently sound out the word. Then have students read the sentence. Assist, as needed.

5 GENERALIZATION: READING NEW WORDS IN PARAGRAPHS
- Have students read the paragraph silently, then out loud. Tell students to use the sounds and word parts they know to read any difficult words.
- Repeat practice, as needed.

Science Digest

Unit 17 Exercise 5
Use before The Garden We Share, Chapters 2, 3

1. SOUND REVIEW Have students review sounds for accuracy, then for fluency.

A	aw as in paw	oo as in book	ci as in circle	ph as in phone	oo as in moon
B	all	au	u_e	o_e	ir

2. SOUND PRACTICE In each column, have students spell and say the sound, then say any underlined sound and the word. Next, have them read the column.

ea as in eagle	**ew**	**oo** as in moon	**ai**	Bossy E
br<u>ea</u>the	f<u>ew</u>	s<u>oo</u>n	w<u>ai</u>t	h<u>a</u>te
w<u>ea</u>k	gr<u>ew</u>	br<u>oo</u>m	<u>ai</u>ry	thr<u>i</u>ves
f<u>ea</u>st	dr<u>ew</u>	r<u>oo</u>ts	m<u>ai</u>led	ch<u>a</u>sed

3. ACCURACY/FLUENCY BUILDING For each column, have students say any underlined part, then read each word. Next, have them read the column.

A1 Mixed Practice	**B1** Shifty Words	**C1** Morphographs/Affixes	**D1** Multisyllabic Words	**E1** Tricky Words
p<u>a</u>tch	<u>wa</u>lk	activ<u>ity</u>	han·dles	aphid
fen<u>ce</u>	t<u>a</u>lk	<u>ex</u>plained	rib·bons	nectar
r<u>ow</u>s	st<u>a</u>lk	act<u>or</u>	con·tin·ued	pulling
s<u>oi</u>l	st<u>a</u>lk<u>s</u>	<u>pre</u>view		piece
<u>k</u>now		bold<u>er</u>	handles	
curled		permi<u>ss</u>ion	ribbons	
<u>a</u>greed			continued	
enj<u>oy</u>				

TEACH TO MASTERY/ DISCRIMINATION PRACTICE

Repeated Practice

Provide repeated practice on each task. If you hear an error, gently correct the whole group with a demonstration and/or guided practice. Move to another skill or task, then return to the difficult item many times—mixing group and individual turns, independent of your voice. When a task is easy, build speed of recognition.

Remember, practice makes perfect! And practice builds fluency.

4. WORDS IN CONTEXT Have students use the sounds and word parts they know to figure out the word. Then have them read the sentence.

A	bush	Josephine shrieked when she discovered beetles on her rose <u>bush</u>.
B	cam·ou·flaged	Nate noticed many insects <u>camouflaged</u> by the plants.

5. GENERALIZATION Have students read the paragraph silently, then out loud. (New words: Mrs. Chen, tended, weeding, sunflowers, Ladybugs, harvested)

   Mrs. Chen had the most beautiful garden in the neighborhood. She tended to her garden every day. You could see her weeding and watering right on schedule. She grew pretty sunflowers, lettuce, and tomatoes. Ladybugs, butterflies, and robins visited her garden. Whenever she harvested her lettuce, she gave some to my rabbit to nibble on.

CHAPTER 2 INSTRUCTIONS

Students read Chapter 2, pages 56–58, with the teacher. Students read Chapter 3, pages 59–61 on their own during their independent work.

COMPREHENSION PROCESSES

Remember, Understand, Apply, Evaluate, Create

PROCEDURES

1. Reviewing Chapter 1

Identifying—Narrator, Problem, Main Character, Goal;
Using Vocabulary—vacant

Have students review the questions from Chapter 1, Setting a Purpose.

Who is telling the story? (Cara is telling the story.) Yes, Cara is the narrator.

What is the problem? (The vacant lot is a mess. It makes her mother sad.)

What did the main character want? What was her goal?

(Cara wanted to get the neighbors to help her clean the vacant lot.)

2. Introducing Chapter 2

Identifying—What; Predicting; Making Judgments; Generating Ideas;
Using Vocabulary—community

Say something like:

At the end of Chapter 1, everyone agrees that the vacant lot is a perfect spot for a . . . (garden).

What do you think the community will do? (They will plant a garden.)

Do you think it's a good idea to plant a garden in the lot? Why or why not?

(Yes, they can grow food to eat and flowers to make it pretty. No, it would be hard to take care of it . . .)

What else could the neighbors do with the lot? (They could build a playground for the kids. They could start a farm. They could build a community center . . .)

3. First Reading

- Ask questions and discuss the story as indicated by the gray text.
- Mix group and individual turns, independent of your voice.
  Have students work toward a group accuracy goal of 0–2 errors.
  Quietly keep track of errors made by all students in the group.
- After reading the story, practice any difficult words.
  Repeat if students have not reached the accuracy goal.

4. Second Reading, Short Passage Practice: Developing Prosody

- Demonstrate expressive, fluent reading on the first paragraph.
  Read at a rate slightly faster than the students' rate.
- Guide practice with your voice.
- Provide individual turns while others track with their fingers and whisper read.
- Repeat steps with each remaining paragraph.

WITH THE TEACHER

Chapter 2

The Garden Thrives

Who is the story about?**1**
What did the neighbors decide to do?**2**

The neighbors helped turn the dirt, make rows, plant seeds, and water the plants. We set up a schedule for taking care of the garden.

56

COMPREHENDING AS YOU GO

1 **Remember:** Identifying—Main Characters (The story is about Cara and her neighbors.)

2 **Understand:** Explaining—Event; Using Vocabulary—vacant (The neighbors decided to plant a garden in the vacant lot.)

THE GARDEN WE SHARE

In a few weeks, our community garden was thriving. Neat rows of lettuce grew like pretty green ribbons. Bean stalks curled up around old broom handles.

One day, as I was pulling weeds from the garden, I found some worms squirming in the dirt. I held one up to Josephine. "Ewww!" she shrieked. "I hate worms."

"Worms are good for our garden," explained Mrs. Chen. "They help make the soil soft so the roots can grow. They turn the dirt and make it airy so the roots can breathe."

I carefully put the worm back in the dirt and continued weeding.

As Josephine and I weeded, we noticed some rabbits sitting under a bush. They had one eye on us and one eye on the lettuce.

Everyone loved our garden in the lot. Butterflies and bees drank sweet nectar from the flowers. Robins ate worms. Other birds munched on beetles and ate sunflower seeds.

Why do you think the rabbits are interested in the garden?1
Why did Cara carefully put the worm back in the garden?2

57

COMPREHENDING AS YOU GO

❶ **Apply:** Inferring, Explaining (The rabbits are hungry. The rabbits want to eat the lettuce . . .)

❷ **Apply:** Inferring, Explaining (Cara put the worm back because it is good for the garden. Worms make the soil soft so the roots can grow. Worms eat dead stuff and break it down into nutrients for the plants.)

5. Think and Talk

- Ask and discuss each question with your group.
- For items 5 and 6, have students work in partners. Say something like:
  For the next question, we're going to work in partners.

  Remember to:
  1. Listen to your partner.
  2. Whisper to each other.

  Listen to the next question, "Why did Cara put the worm back?" Partner A, tell your partner why Cara put the worm back.

  Wait, then say something like:
  Partner B, add to your partner's answer. Why did Cara put the worm back?
  Wait, then discuss answers with the group.
  Let's all talk about our answers. [Emily], how did you and your partner answer the question?
  (Cara put the worm back because it is good for the garden.)
  Repeat for Question 6.

WITH THE TEACHER

Think and Talk

SETTING
1. Where does the story take place?

MAIN CHARACTER, GOAL
2. Who is the main character, and what did she want?

ACTION
3. What was her "awesome plan"?

ACTION
4. What did the neighbors do?

INFERENCE
5. Why did Cara put the worm back?

DESCRIPTION
6. Describe the garden.

❶ **Remember:** Identifying—Setting (The story takes place in Cara's neighborhood.)

❷ **Remember:** Identifying—Main Character, Goal; Using Vocabulary—vacant (Cara is the main character. She wanted to clean up the vacant lot.)

❸ **Understand:** Explaining (Her plan was to ask the neighbors to help clean up the lot.)

❹ **Understand:** Explaining—Action (The neighbors came and cleaned up the lot. Then they planted a garden. They took care of the garden.)

❺ **Apply:** Inferring, Explaining (Cara put the worm back because it is good for the garden. The worm makes the soil soft so the roots can grow. Worms eat dead stuff and break it down into nutrients for the plants.)

❻ **Understand:** Describing; Using Vocabulary—thriving (The garden is thriving. There are rows of lettuce and bean stalks. Butterflies and bees like the flowers. The birds like the worms and sunflower seeds.)

CHAPTER 3 INSTRUCTIONS

Students read pages 59–61 without the teacher, independently or with partners.

COMPREHENSION PROCESSES

Remember, Understand, Apply, Evaluate, Create

PROCEDURES FOR READING ON YOUR OWN

1. Getting Ready

Have students turn to Chapter 3, "Something for Everyone," on page 59.

2. Setting a Purpose

Identifying—Problem, Solution; Responding; Generating Ideas

Before students begin reading, say something like:

This is the last chapter of our story. Let's read to find out how the story ends. Think about the answer to these questions as you read:

- What problems do Cara and the neighbors have in the garden?
- How do they solve the problems?
- Do you think their solutions are good ones? What else could they have done to solve the problems?

> **PREP NOTE**
>
> **Setting a Purpose**
>
> Write questions on a chalkboard, white board, or large piece of paper before working with your small group.

3. Reading on Your Own: Partner or Whisper Reading

- Have students take turns reading every other page with a partner or have students whisper read pages 59–61 on their own.
- Continue having students track each word with their fingers.
- Have students ask themselves or their partners the gray text questions.

4. Comprehension and Skill Work

Tell students that they will do Comprehension and Skill Activities 9, 10a, and 10b after they read on their own. Guide practice, as needed. For teacher directions, see pages 105–107. If you are on an 8- to 11-Day Plan, students will have additional time to complete Comprehension and Skill Activities 10a and 10b in the next lesson.

5. Homework 5: Repeated Reading

ON YOUR OWN

Chapter 3
Something for Everyone

Every day, the neighbors tended the garden. One day, we discovered that there were insects called aphids eating some of the plants. We could hardly see the tiny green bugs. "We should get rid of them," said Mrs. Knight. "Aphids make the plants weak."

"We can get some ladybugs," said Mrs. Chen. "Ladybugs eat aphids, and they won't eat our plants or harm anything else. I know exactly where to get ladybugs."

What is the problem in the garden?1
How do aphids protect themselves?2

59

COMPREHENDING
AS YOU GO

❶ **Understand:** Explaining—Problem (Aphids are eating some of the plants.)

❷ **Apply:** Inferring, Explaining (Aphids are tiny and green, so they are hard to see on the plants.)

ON YOUR OWN

Mrs. Chen mailed away for the ladybugs. They came all wrapped up in a big ball. We let the ladybugs go in the garden. They chased around eating up the aphids. Soon our aphid problem was solved.

A few days later, we had a new problem. The rabbits had become bolder. They were making a feast of our lettuce and beans!

How did the gardeners solve their problem?[1]
What is the new problem?[2]
What do you think the gardeners should do?[3]

COMPREHENDING AS YOU GO

❶ Understand: Explaining—Solution (They solved the problem by sending away for ladybugs to eat the aphids.)

❷ Remember: Identifying—Problem (The new problem is that the rabbits are eating the lettuce and beans.)

❸ Create: Generating Ideas (The gardeners could scare the rabbits so they run away. They could catch the rabbits and let them go somewhere else . . .)

THE GARDEN WE SHARE

"I have an idea," said Mr. Phillips. "We can build a fence around our garden."

Everyone got busy. The rabbits watched as we worked on the fence. Soon it was almost done.

"Wait," I said. "This garden is for the whole neighborhood. The people all enjoy it. So do the birds and butterflies. Could we leave a little piece of garden for the rabbits?"

We agreed to leave a little patch with no fence, so the rabbits could nibble on their own lettuce and beans.

Now we have a beautiful garden to harvest, and the rabbits have a little garden too. I like the garden we share.

What did the neighbors do to protect their garden?**1**
How did they share the garden with the rabbits?**2**
Do you think this was a good solution?**3**

61

COMPREHENDING
AS YOU GO

1 **Understand:** Explaining; Using Vocabulary—protect (The neighbors built a fence around the garden to protect it from the rabbits.)

2 **Understand:** Explaining—Solution (They left part of the garden with no fence so the rabbits could eat too.)

3 **Evaluate:** Making Judgments (This was a good solution because the rabbits and people are both happy. This was a bad solution because more rabbits will come, so the neighbors will need to grow more food for them.)

JUST FOR FUN • WRITE A RIDDLE

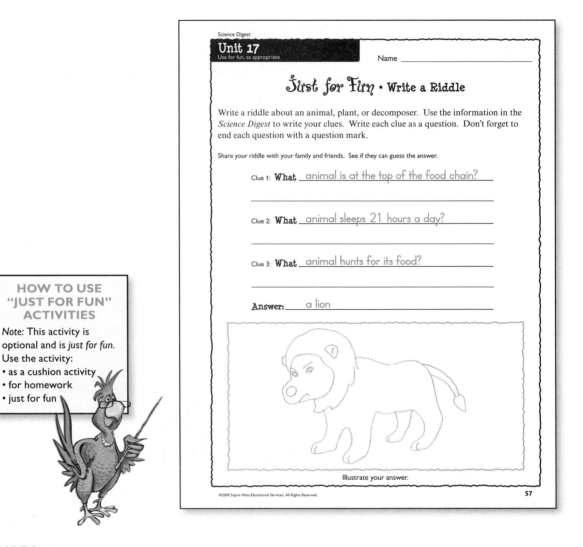

HOW TO USE "JUST FOR FUN" ACTIVITIES

Note: This activity is optional and is *just for fun.* Use the activity:
• as a cushion activity
• for homework
• just for fun

PROCEDURES

As time allows, have students write a riddle about an animal, plant, or decomposer. Students can then illustrate the answer to the riddle.

This page may be given to students as homework.

Sentence/Question Completion, Illustrating—Specific Instructions
• Have students read the directions, then complete the questions. Remind students to start with a capital and end with a question mark.
• Have students write the answer to their riddle.
• Have students illustrate the answer to their riddle.

STORY MAP

COMPREHENSION PROCESSES

Understand, Apply

WRITING TRAITS

Conventions—Capital

Using Graphic Organizer
Summarizing, Sequencing

Identifying—Setting, Narrator

Explaining—Beginning,
Initiating Event, Problem, Goal

Explaining—Middle, Action, Solution
Sequencing—Events
Using Vocabulary—vacant, thrive

Explaining—End, Outcome/Conclusion

Science Digest

Unit 17 Activity 9
Use after Exercise 5 and The Garden We Share.
Chapters 2 and 3

Name _____

Story Map
The Garden We Share

If you need to, look in your storybook.

◆ **INTRODUCTION**

| Setting | Where | in a city |
| Narrator | Who | Cara |

● **BEGINNING**

Initiating Event
Problem — messy vacant lot

Goal — Cara's Plan — to make the lot into a garden

■ **MIDDLE**

Action

Neighbors — cleaned up trash, raked, planted seeds

Garden — thrived

Aphid Problem/Solution — ordered ladybugs

Rabbit Problem/Solution — built fence, made a rabbit garden

▲ **END**

Outcome/
Conclusion — • a beautiful garden to share

58

©2009 Sopris West Educational Services. All Rights Reserved.

PROCEDURES

Use an overhead BLM copy of the story map to demonstrate and guide practice, as needed.

Story Map: Phrases—Specific Instructions

• Have students complete the map.
• Guide, as needed. For the beginning, say something like:

Let's discuss what happened at the beginning of the story. What was the problem? (There was a messy vacant lot.)

What could you write next to "Problem"? (messy, vacant lot)

What was Cara's plan? (to make the vacant lot into a garden)

What could you write? (to make the lot into a garden, to clean the lot and make a garden . . .)

For the middle, say something like:

Let's discuss the middle, the action. Read the word in the next box. (Neighbors)

What did the neighbors do? (cleaned the lot, raked the dirt, made a garden)

What short phrases could you write in the box? (cleaned, raked, planted seeds . . .)

Read the word in the next box. (Garden)

Tell something about the garden. Use the word *thrived*. (The garden thrived. Things grew well . . .)

Repeat as needed for "Aphid Problem/Solution" and "Rabbit Problem/Solution."

• For some groups, provide students with time to complete each section. Then guide the next section.

WRITTEN RETELL

COMPREHENSION PROCESSES

Remember, Understand, Apply, Evaluate

WRITING TRAITS

**Organization—Sequencing
Conventions—Complete Sentence,
Capital, Period
Presentation**

Summarizing, Sequencing

Identifying—Setting, Narrator

Explaining—Beginning,
Initiating Event, Problem, Goal

Explaining—Middle, Action, Solution

Science Digest

Unit 17 Activity **10a**
Use after Exercise 5 and The Garden We Share,
Chapters 2 and 3

Name _____

Written Retell
The Garden We Share

◆ **INTRODUCTION • Setting/Narrator**
Tell where the story takes place and who is telling the story.

This story takes place in a city. A young girl named
Cara is telling the story.

● **BEGINNING • Initiating Event:** Describe the problem and the narrator's goal.

At the beginning of the story, Cara's mom said the vacant lot
was a mess. Cara had a great plan. She wanted to make the
lot into a garden.

■ **MIDDLE • Action**
Write what the neighbors did to the vacant lot. Describe the garden.
Explain how the aphid and rabbit problems were solved.

First, the neighbors got together. Then they cleaned,
raked, and planted seeds. They spiffed up the lot!

Soon the garden thrived. All kinds of vegetables grew in the
garden—lettuce, tomatoes, and sunflowers.

59

PROCEDURES

Use an overhead BLM copy of the
story map to demonstrate and guide
how to create a written retell. Provide
only as much support as your students
need to be successful. Suggested
options include:

• Entire Written Retell: Demonstrate and guide how to write a section of the retell. Then
provide time for students to complete that section before guiding the next section.

• Selected Section(s): Demonstrate and guide only those sections that are the most difficult for
your students (see below). Then have students write their own retells.

• Oral Discussion: Brainstorm possible responses and have students complete the retell on
their own.

Written Retell: Paragraph Writing—Specific Instructions

• Guide how to use the story map from Activity 9 to complete the middle section of the retell.
Say something like:

For the middle part of the story, we're going to write about the action. Find the square.
Read the directions in the gray bar. (Write what the neighbors did to the vacant lot . . .)
Wow! It's a good thing we have our story maps to help us. The first thing we need to write is
what the neighbors did. My map says the neighbors "cleaned up trash, raked, planted seeds."

(continued)

WRITTEN RETELL (*continued*)

Summarizing, Sequencing

Explaining—End, Outcome/Conclusion

Responding

Visualizing, Illustrating

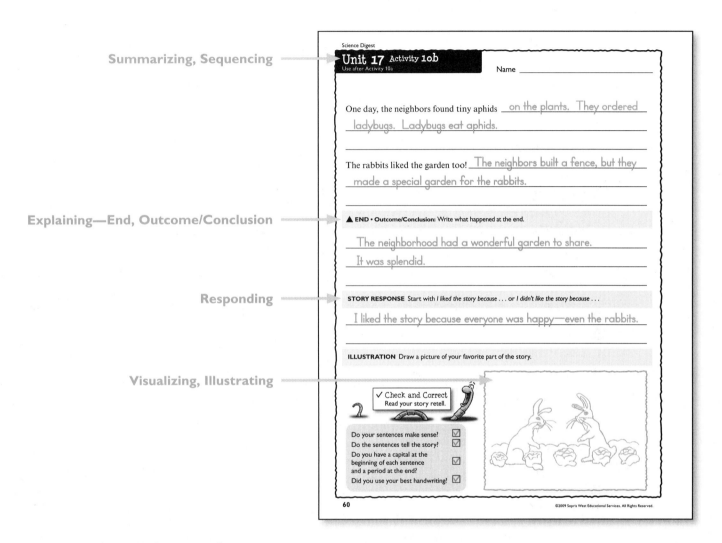

Science Digest

Unit 17 Activity **1ob**
Use after Activity 10a

Name _____

One day, the neighbors found tiny aphids __on the plants. They ordered__ __ladybugs. Ladybugs eat aphids.__

_____

The rabbits liked the garden too! __The neighbors built a fence, but they__ __made a special garden for the rabbits.__

_____

▲ **END • Outcome/Conclusion:** Write what happened at the end.

__The neighborhood had a wonderful garden to share.__
__It was splendid.__

STORY RESPONSE Start with *I liked the story because . . .* or *I didn't like the story because . . .*

__I liked the story because everyone was happy—even the rabbits.__

ILLUSTRATION Draw a picture of your favorite part of the story.

✓ Check and Correct
Read your story retell.

Do your sentences make sense? ☑
Do the sentences tell the story? ☑
Do you have a capital at the beginning of each sentence and a period at the end? ☑
Did you use your best handwriting? ☑

60

©2009 Sopris West Educational Services. All Rights Reserved.

Written Retell (*continued*)

- Demonstrate writing. Say something like:

  Our retell starts with "First," so I could write, "They cleaned up trash, raked leaves, and planted seeds."

  Hmmm . . . That's kind of boring so I think I'll write a little more.

  I think I'll write, "First, the neighbors got together and planned the garden. Then they cleaned, raked, and planted leaves." I like that better!

- Have students suggest other options.

  What else could we write? [John], what might you write? Start with "First." (First, the neighbors got together and spiffed up the vacant lot.) Oh, that's even better.

- Repeat with each part of the middle, as needed.

- Have students complete the retell and illustration.

Self-monitoring

Have students use the Check and Correct box to evaluate and fix their work, as needed.

❶ SOUND REVIEW

Have students read the sounds and key word phrases in each row. Work for accuracy, then fluency.

❷ ACCURACY AND FLUENCY BUILDING

- For each task, have students say any underlined part, then read the word.
- Set a pace. Then have students read the whole words in each task and column.
- Provide repeated practice, building accuracy first, then fluency.

D1. Word Endings

Have students read the underlined word, then the word with an ending.

Note: Tell students you double the t when you add -ed to "rot."

E1. Tricky Words

- For each Tricky Word, have students use the sounds and word parts they know to silently sound out the word. Use the word in a sentence to help with pronunciation.

died	Amanda cried when her pet turtle . . . *died.*
heard	The song was an oldie that we had . . . *heard* . . . before.
hours	One day is equal to 24 . . . *hours.*
whole	He didn't want the sandwich cut in half. He wanted it . . . *whole.*
once	He climbed the ladder only one time. He climbed it . . . *once.*

- Have students go back and read the whole words in the column.

❸ MORPHOGRAPHS AND AFFIXES

- Have students read the underlined part, then the word.
- Repeat practice with whole words, mixing group and individual turns.
  Build accuracy, then fluency.
- For the word "reuse," review the meaning of the morphograph.
  Say something like: What does re- mean? (again) *Reuse* means use . . . again.

❹ GENERALIZATION: READING NEW WORDS IN PARAGRAPHS

- Have students read the paragraph silently, then out loud. Tell students to use the sounds and word parts they know to read any difficult words.
- Repeat practice, as needed.

Fluency

Unit 17 Exercise 6
Use before Links in a Food Chain

1. SOUND REVIEW Have students review sounds for accuracy, then for fluency.

A	-y as in fly	-y as in baby	oy as in boy	ci as in circle	au as in astronaut
B	ph	oa	ou	-dge	igh

2. ACCURACY/FLUENCY BUILDING For each column, have students say any underlined part, then read each word. Next, have them read the column.

A1 Mixed Practice	B1 Mixed Practice	C1 Shifty Words	D1 Word Endings	E1 Tricky Words
giraffe	soil	link	rotted	died
Austin	grew	slink	flowers	heard
elephant	snake	sling	gobbled	hours
ledge	chain	spring	nibbled	whole
awful	grow			once
digest	roast			
knock	circle			

3. MORPHOGRAPHS AND AFFIXES Have students read the underlined word part, then the word.

A	ability	possibly	apartment	distance	reuse
B	collector	possible	discussion	excite	nomadic

4. GENERALIZATION Have students read the paragraph silently, then out loud. (New words: swallowed, creepies, crawlies, slimies)

There are creepy bugs, crawly insects, and slimy earthworms and slugs in our garden. Although most people may shriek at the sight of these bugs, worms, and slugs, I think they are cool. One day, I had my mouth open and almost swallowed a bug. I thought that was funny. I love those creepies, crawlies, and slimies.

42

FLUENCY PASSAGE INSTRUCTIONS

This Story Reading targets fluency as the primary goal of instruction and practice. Students do repeated readings of this poem to improve accuracy, expression, and rate.

PROCEDURES

1. **Warm-Up: Partner Reading or Whisper Reading**
   Before beginning group Story Reading, have students finger track and partner or whisper read the selection.

2. **First Reading**
   - Mix group and individual turns, independent of your voice. Have students work toward a group accuracy goal of 0–2 errors. Quietly keep track of errors made by all students in the group.
   - After reading the story, practice any difficult words. Reread the story if students have not reached the accuracy goal.

3. **Second Reading, Short Passage Practice: Developing Prosody**
   - Demonstrate reading the first stanza with expression and fluency. Have students finger track as you read.
   - Have students choral read the first stanza. Encourage reading with expression and fluency.
   - Repeat with second stanza.

4. **Third Reading, Group Timed Readings: Repeated Reading**

   - Select a page. Encourage each child to work for a personal best. Have students whisper read for a one-minute Timed Reading. Tell students to go back to the top of the page and keep reading until the minute is up.
   - Have students put their finger on the last word they read and count the number of words read correctly in one minute.
   - Have students do a second Timed Reading of the same page.
   - Have students try to beat their last score.
   - Celebrate improvements.

5. **Written Assessment (Comprehension and Skill)**
   Tell students they will do a Written Assessment after they read "Links in a Food Chain." (For teacher directions, see pages 115 and 116.)

6. **Homework 6: Repeated Reading**

WITH THE TEACHER

Fluency

Links in a Food Chain

Author Unknown
illustrated by Tatjana Mai-Wyss

There once was a flower that grew on the plain,   10
Where the sun helped it grow, and so did the rain,   21
Links in a food chain.   26

There once was a bug who nibbled on flowers,   35
Nibbled on flowers for hours and hours!   42

The bug ate the flower that grew on the plain,   52
Where the sun helped it grow, and so did the rain,   63
Links in a food chain.   68

LINKS IN A FOOD CHAIN

There once was a bird who gobbled up bugs,   9
And creepies and crawlies and slimies and slugs.   17

The bird ate the bug who nibbled on flowers,   26
Nibbled on flowers for hours and hours!   33

The bug ate the flower that grew on the plain,   43
Where the sun helped it grow, and so did the rain,   54
Links in a food chain.   59

There once was a snake who often grabbed birds,   68
And swallowed them whole, or so I have heard.   77

The snake ate the bird who gobbled up bugs,   86
And creepies and crawlies and slimies and slugs.   94

The bird ate the bug who nibbled on flowers,   103
Nibbled on flowers for hours and hours!   110

The bug ate the flower that grew on the plain,   120
Where the sun helped it grow, and so did the rain,   131
Links in a food chain.   136

63

WITH THE TEACHER

Fluency

There once was a fox, and I'll make a bet;   10
He'd eat anything he could possibly get.   17

The fox ate the snake who often grabbed birds,   26
and swallowed them whole, or so I have heard.   35

The snake ate the bird who gobbled up bugs,   44
And creepies and crawlies and slimies and slugs.   52

The bird ate the bug who nibbled on flowers,   61
Nibbled on flowers for hours and hours!   68

The bug ate the flower that grew on the plain,   78
Where the sun helped it grow, and so did the rain,   89
Links in a food chain.   94

64

LINKS IN A FOOD CHAIN

The fox, he grew older and died one spring day,   10
But he made the soil rich when he rotted away.   20

A new flower grew where he died on the plain.   30
And the sun helped it grow, and so did the rain,   41
Links in a food chain.   46

This poem can be sung to the tune of *I Know an Old Woman Who Swallowed a Fly.*

65

WRITTEN ASSESSMENT (1 of 2)

COMPREHENSION PROCESSES

Remember, Understand, Apply

WRITING TRAITS

Organization—Topic Sentence, Supporting Details
Conventions—Complete Sentence, Capital, Period
Presentation

Test Taking
Using Vocabulary—food chain

Identifying—Main Idea

Using Graphic Organizer—Hierarchy
Identifying—Supporting Details/Facts

Summarizing—Facts
Paragraph Writing

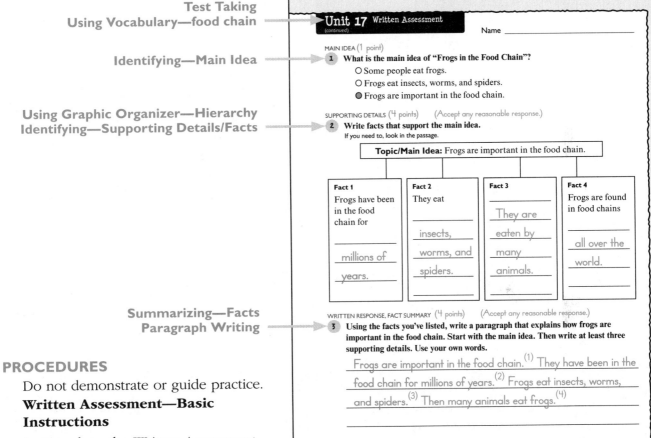

PROCEDURES

Do not demonstrate or guide practice.
Written Assessment—Basic
Instructions

1. Introduce the Written Assessment.
   Tell students they will whisper read
   the passage and then answer the
   questions without help.

   Today is our Written Assessment day.

   You get to show me what you can do on your own. First, whisper read the passage and then
   answer the questions—just like you've been doing on your Comprehension and Skill Work.

   If you read a question and aren't sure what to do, what should you do?

   (Reread the question and try again.)

   If you still can't answer the question, what should you do?

   (Reread the passage and try again.)

   If you still aren't sure, I know you will do your best.

WRITTEN ASSESSMENT (2 of 2)

Comprehension Monitoring

Using Vocabulary—energy
Making Connections

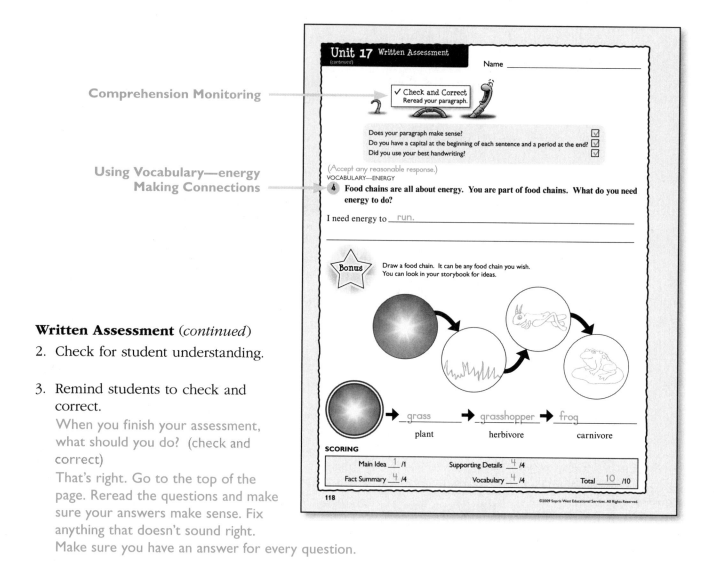

Written Assessment (*continued*)

2. Check for student understanding.

3. Remind students to check and correct.

   When you finish your assessment, what should you do? (check and correct)

   That's right. Go to the top of the page. Reread the questions and make sure your answers make sense. Fix anything that doesn't sound right.

   Make sure you have an answer for every question.

4. Remind students what to do when they finish their work.

End of the Unit

In this section, you will find:

Making Decisions

As you near the end of the unit, plan to give the Written Assessment and the Oral Reading Fluency Assessment to each child in your group. Use this section as a general guide for making instructional decisions and doing diagnostic planning.

Written Assessment

The Unit 17 Written Assessment is located on page 115 of *Activity Book 3* and on the CD.

Oral Reading Fluency Assessment

The Unit 17 Oral Reading Fluency Assessment is located on page 121 of this teacher's guide and in the *Assessment Manual*.

Certificate of Achievement

Celebrate your children's accomplishments. When your students master the unit skills, send home the Certificate of Achievement.

Goal Setting

Through goal setting, help your students recognize their accomplishments and learn how to be self-directed learners.

Extra Practice Lessons

Use the Extra Practice lessons for students who need additional decoding and fluency work. Student materials can be copied from the Extra Practice blackline masters.

Making Decisions

1. After students read Story Reading 6, "Links in a Food Chain," give the group the Unit 17 Written Assessment in place of Comprehension and Skill Work. Follow the instructions on pages 115 and 116 of this guide.

2. While the group is completing the Written Assessment or any time during the day, administer the Oral Reading Fluency Assessment. Assess each student individually.

   Optional: Graph the results of the assessment. (See Unit 7 Teacher's Guide, pages 92 and 95.)
   • If the student's words correct per minute go up, congratulate the student.
   • If the student's words correct per minute go down, discuss the student's overall improvement and help him or her identify ways to improve for the next assessment.

3. Score oral fluency responses on the Student Assessment Record. Adhere to the scoring criteria in the *Assessment Manual*. Use a stopwatch to time how long it takes each student to read the Oral Reading Fluency Passage, and record errors.

USING WRITTEN ASSESSMENT RESULTS

Results of the Written Assessment *should not* be used to determine whether a student or group of students continues forward in the program. As long as students pass the Oral Reading Fluency Assessment, they should continue forward with the next unit.

The Written Assessment should be used to informally monitor how well students read independently and answer questions in writing. If any student has difficulty with the Written Assessment, re-administer the assessment orally.

If the student has difficulty answering the questions orally:
• Record the types of errors (e.g., main idea, sequencing, open-ended response).
• Provide explicit instruction for these types of questions during reading group, before independent work, and in tutorials, as needed.
  1) Demonstrate (or model) appropriate responses, guide practice, and provide opportunities for independent practice.
  2) For inferential questions, think aloud with students—explain how you arrive at an answer.
  3) For literal questions, teach students to reread a passage, locate information, reread the question, and respond.

USING THE ORAL READING FLUENCY RESULTS

At the end of each unit, you will need to make decisions regarding student progress. Should students go forward in the program? Does the group need Extra Practice before proceeding? Do individuals require more assistance and practice to continue working in their group? These decisions all require use of the oral reading fluency data and professional judgment. As you analyze assessment results, watch for trends and anomalies.

See the *Assessment Manual* for detailed information and instructional recommendations. General guidelines and recommendations follow:

Strong Pass ≥ 119 WCPM 0–2 errors	• Continue with the current pace of instruction. • Have students set goals. (Until students are reading approximately 180 words correct per minute, oral reading fluency continues to be an instructional goal.)
Pass 98–118 WCPM 0–2 errors	• Continue with the current pace of instruction. Consider increasing fluency practice.
No Pass ≤ 97 WCPM RED FLAG A No Pass is a red flag. A mild early intervention can prevent an intense and time-consuming intervention in the future.	• If a child scores a No Pass but has previously passed all assessments, you may wish to advance the student to the next unit, then carefully monitor the student. • If a child scores a No Pass but has previously passed all assessments, you may wish to advance the student to the next unit and also provide additional practice opportunities. (See below.) • If a child scores two consecutive No Passes or periodic No Passes, additional practice must be provided. (See below.) • If a child scores three consecutive No Passes, the student should be placed in a lower-performing group.

Added Practice Options for Groups

Warm-Ups:
- Begin each lesson with Partner Reading of the previous day's homework.
- Begin each day with Partner Reading of a Word Fluency from Extra Practice.
- Begin each lesson with a five-minute Fluency Booster. Place copies of the Unit 7–16 *Read Well* Homework in three-ring notebooks. Each day, have students begin Finger Tracking and Whisper Reading at Unit 7, Homework 1. At the end of five minutes, have students mark where they are in their notebooks. The next day, the goal is to read farther.
- Begin each Story Reading with a review of the previous day's story.
- After reading the story, include Short Passage Practice on a daily basis.

Extended Units: If several children begin to score No Passes or barely pass, extend the unit by adding Extra Practices 1, 2, and/or 3. Extra Practice lessons include Decoding Practice, Fluency Passage, Word Fluency, and a Comprehension and Skill Activity. (See pages 124–132 in this guide.)

Jell-Well Reviews: A Jell-Well Review is the *Read Well* term for a review of earlier units. A Jell-Well Review is a period of time taken to celebrate what children have learned and an opportunity to firm up their foundation of learning. To complete a Jell-Well Review, take the group back to the last unit for which all students scored Strong Passes. Then quickly cycle up again. See the *Assessment Manual* for how to build a Jell-Well Review.

Added Practice Options for Individual Students

Tutorials: Set up five-minute tutorials on a daily basis with an assistant, trained volunteer, or cross-age tutor. Have the tutor provide Short Passage Practice and Timed Readings or Extra Practice lessons.

Double Dose: Find ways to provide a double dose of *Read Well* instruction.

• Have the student work in his or her group *and* a lower-performing group.

• Have an instructional assistant, older student, or parent volunteer preview or review lessons.

• Have an instructional assistant provide instruction with Extra Practice lessons.

• Preview new lessons or review previous lessons.

END-OF-THE-UNIT CELEBRATION

When students pass the Oral Reading Fluency Assessment, celebrate with the Certificate of Achievement on p. 122.

Note: Using the Flesch-Kincaid Grade Level readability formula, the Unit 17 Assessment has a 2.9 readability level. Readabilities are based on number of words per sentence and number of syllables per word. Adding one or two multisyllabic words can increase readability by a month or two. Though we are attending to readability for the assessments, the overriding factor is decodability.

GOAL SETTING

If you choose to have students set goals:

• Copy a goal-setting form from page 123 for each student and write in students' names.

• For each student, fill in the number of words correct per minute improvement goal for the next unit (2 words per second).

• Guide students through the form. Say something like:

Read the sentence under "My Goals." (I'm a powerful reader. I read a science magazine about food chains.)

You are powerful readers. It is impressive that you can read such sophisticated information!

Look at the box. It tells you what your fluency was for Unit 17. It also tells you how many words you've improved by since the beginning of the year. [Jan], how many words have you improved by? (30)

Wow! That is very, very impressive.

[Jasmine], what does "impressive" mean? (It means that I should be proud of myself.)

Yes, that's exactly right. You've all made great gains, and you should be proud of yourselves.

Everyone find your personal goal for Unit 18. The last part of the form is the most important. It tells what you can do to reach your personal goal. Let's read what you can do.

• Help students be in control of their progress by helping them identify what actions they can take to meet their goal.

predators	prey	listened	zebra	watched	western

At the Water Hole

★The day was coming to an end. The hot sun was finally   12
setting in the western sky. All day long, the zebra herd grazed on   25
dry grass. The lion pride spent the day sleeping in the shade of a   39
big tree. Now all the animals needed to drink.   48

    The lions stood up slowly, one by one, and began walking   59
to the water hole. Their giant paws made no sound on the dusty   72
ground. They were predators, at the top of the food chain. They   84
had nothing to fear.   88

    The zebras also walked slowly to the water hole. They   98
were prey animals. They watched and listened for predators.   107
They were ready to run if there was danger.   116

    The zebras and lions came together at the water hole. The   127
lions were not hungry. They would hunt tomorrow. The zebras   137
were safe. They all took turns drinking the cool, clear water.   148

ORAL READING FLUENCY	Start timing at the ★ Mark errors. Make a single slash in the text (/) at 60 seconds. Have the student complete the passage. If the student completes the passage in less than 60 seconds, have the student go back to the ★ and continue reading. Make a double slash in the text (//) at 60 seconds.
WCPM	Determine words correct per minute by subtracting errors from words read in 60 seconds.
STRONG PASS	The student scores no more than 2 errors on the first pass through the passage and reads 119 or more words correct per minute. Proceed to Unit 18.
PASS	The student scores no more than 2 errors on the first pass through the passage and reads 98 to 118 words correct per minute. Proceed to Unit 18.
NO PASS	The student scores 3 or more errors on the first pass through the passage and/or reads 97 or fewer words correct per minute. Provide added fluency practice with *RW2* Unit 17 Extra Practice. (Lessons follow the certificate at the end of the teacher's guide.) After completing the Extra Practice, retest the student.

A Thriving Reader!

_____

has successfully completed

Read Well 2 Unit 17 • Science Digest: Food Chains

with _____ words correct per minute.

Teacher Signature _____

Date _____

✂ -

A Thriving Reader!

_____

has successfully completed

Read Well 2 Unit 17 • Science Digest: Food Chains

with _____ words correct per minute.

Teacher Signature _____

Date _____

My Goals

I am a powerful reader. I read a science magazine about food chains.

My goal for Unit 18 is _____ words correct per minute.

I can work to reach my goal by:

- Reading and rereading carefully
- Working hard in reading group
- _____
  _____

Signed _____

Date _____

My Personal Best:

In Unit 17, I read _____ words correct per minute.

Since the beginning of the year, I've improved my reading by _____ words per minute.

My Goals

I am a powerful reader. I read a science magazine about food chains.

My goal for Unit 18 is _____ words correct per minute.

I can work to reach my goal by:

- Reading and rereading carefully
- Working hard in reading group
- _____
  _____

Signed _____

Date _____

My Personal Best:

In Unit 17, I read _____ words correct per minute.

Since the beginning of the year, I've improved my reading by _____ words per minute.

PROCEDURES

1. **Sound Review**
   Use selected Sound Cards from Units 1–17.

2. **Sounding Out Smoothly**
   - For each word, have students say the underlined part, sound out the word smoothly, then read the whole word. Use the words in sentences, as needed.
   - Have students read all the words in the row, building accuracy first, then fluency.
   - Repeat practice. Mix group and individual turns, independent of your voice.

3. **Accuracy and Fluency Building**
   - For each task, have students say any underlined part, then read each word.
   - Set a pace. Then have students read the whole words in each task and column.
   - Provide repeated practice, building accuracy first, then fluency.

4. **Tricky Words**
   Have students read each row for accuracy, then read the entire grid for fluency.

5. **Multisyllabic Words**
   For each word, have students read each syllable out loud, finger count the syllables, then tell how many syllables are in the word. Have students read the whole word. If needed, use the word in a sentence.

6. **Dictation**
   gave, give, live, brother, mother, another
   - Say "gave." Have students say the word. Guide students as they finger count and say the sounds. Have students touch or write the sounds, then read the word. Say something like:

     The first word is **gave.** Say the word. (gave)

     Say and count the sounds in **gave** with me.

     Hold up one finger for each sound. /g/•/āāā/•/v/ How many sounds? (three)

     What's the first sound? (/g/) Touch under /g/.

     What's the next sound? (/āāā/) Write /āāā/.

     What's the last sound? (/v/) Touch under /v/.

     Read the word. (gave)

     Yes, the Bossy E at the end makes letter a say its name.

   - Repeat with "give" and "live."
   - Continue with the rhyming words: brother, mother, another.

EXTRA PRACTICE 1

Unit 17 Decoding Practice

Name _____

1. SOUND REVIEW Use selected Sound Cards from Units 1–17.

2. SOUNDING OUT SMOOTHLY Have students say the underlined part, sound out and read each word, then read the row.

b<u>or</u>n	<u>ea</u>ch	l<u>oo</u>se	scrat<u>ch</u>

3. ACCURACY/FLUENCY BUILDING Have students say any underlined part, then read each word. Next, have students read the column.

A1 Sound Practice	**B1** Word Endings	**C1** Rhyming Words	**D1** Buildups
angr<u>y</u>	family	<u>s</u>ound	m<u>a</u>d
hungr<u>y</u>	families	<u>gr</u>ound	no<u>mad</u>
bab<u>y</u>		ar<u>ound</u>	no<u>mad</u>ic
memb<u>er</u>	<u>r</u>oaming	**C2** Mixed Practice	c<u>a</u>re
lay<u>er</u>	<u>bark</u>ing	<u>a</u>lso	<u>sc</u>are
aft<u>er</u>	<u>snort</u>ing	nib<u>b</u>le	scar<u>ed</u>
kn<u>ow</u>	sa<u>y</u>ing	hell<u>o</u>	c<u>a</u>pe
sh<u>ow</u>	sleeping	ins<u>e</u>cts	<u>sc</u>ape
sl<u>ow</u>ly	<u>drink</u>ing	<u>a</u>bout	e<u>scape</u>

4. TRICKY WORDS Have students read each row for accuracy, then fluency.

Ⓐ	zebra	group	they	their	pull	5
Ⓑ	move	water	from	hour	want	10

5. MULTISYLLABIC WORDS Have students read the word by parts, tell how many syllables are in the word, then read the whole word.

Ⓐ	with•in	within	to•mor•row	tomorrow
Ⓑ	no•mad•ic	nomadic	pred•a•tor	predator
Ⓒ	pro•tec•tion	protection	com•mu•ni•cate	communicate

6. DICTATION Say the word. Guide students as they say, finger count, and segment the word. Have students say each sound as they touch or write it.

A1 Shifty Words	**B1** Rhyming Words
g<u>a</u>ve	br<u>o</u><u>th</u>er
g<u>i</u>ve	m<u>o</u><u>th</u>er
<u>l</u>ive	an<u>o</u><u>th</u>er

127

PROCEDURES

1. First Reading

Mix group and individual turns, independent of your voice. Have students work toward an accuracy goal of 0–2 errors and practice any difficult words.

2. Second Reading, Short Passage Practice: Developing Prosody

- Demonstrate how to read a line or two with expression. Read at a rate slightly faster than the students' rate. Say something like:

  Listen as I read the first two sentences with expression and phrasing. I'm going to emphasize certain words and pause between sentences.

  "Zebras live in family groups. Zebra families are nomadic, roaming around to find food and water."

- Guide practice with your voice.
  Now read the paragraph with me.

- Provide individual turns while others track with their fingers and whisper read. Provide descriptive, positive feedback.
  [Zan], you read with wonderful expression!

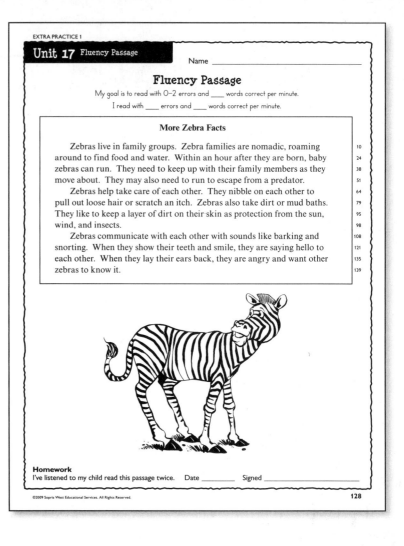

EXTRA PRACTICE 1

Unit 17 Fluency Passage

Name _____

Fluency Passage

My goal is to read with 0–2 errors and ____ words correct per minute.

I read with ____ errors and ____ words correct per minute.

More Zebra Facts

    Zebras live in family groups. Zebra families are nomadic, roaming around to find food and water. Within an hour after they are born, baby zebras can run. They need to keep up with their family members as they move about. They may also need to run to escape from a predator.
    Zebras help take care of each other. They nibble on each other to pull out loose hair or scratch an itch. Zebras also take dirt or mud baths. They like to keep a layer of dirt on their skin as protection from the sun, wind, and insects.
    Zebras communicate with each other with sounds like barking and snorting. When they show their teeth and smile, they are saying hello to each other. When they lay their ears back, they are angry and want other zebras to know it.

10
24
38
51
64
79
95
98
108
121
135
139

Homework
I've listened to my child read this passage twice.   Date _____   Signed _____

©2009 Sopris West Educational Services. All Rights Reserved.   **128**

3. Partner Reading: Repeated Reading (Checkout Opportunity)

While students do Partner Reading, listen to individuals read the passage. Work on accuracy and fluency, as needed.

4. Homework: Repeated Reading

Have students read the story at home.

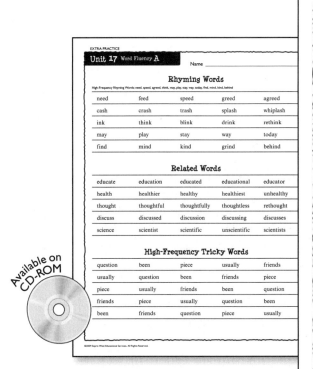

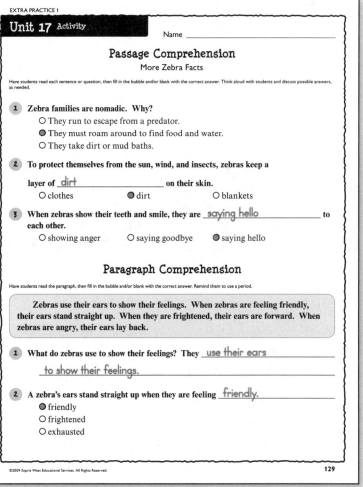

PROCEDURES

For each step, demonstrate and guide practice, as needed. Then have students complete the page independently.

1. Activity

Passage Comprehension
- Have students read each sentence or question, then fill in the bubble and/or blank with the correct answer.
- Think aloud with students and discuss the multiple-choice options, as needed.

Paragraph Comprehension
- Have students read the paragraph.
- Have students read each numbered sentence, then fill in the bubble and/or blank.
- Have students read the completed sentences.

Self-monitoring
Have students read and check their work.

2. Word Fluency (BLMs are located on the CD.)
- To build fluency, have students read Rhyming Words, Related Words, and High-Frequency Tricky Words. Have students read each section three times in a row.
- To build accuracy, have students read all sets with partners.

> **ACCURACY BEFORE FLUENCY**
> **(Reminder)**
> Word Fluency is designed to build accuracy and fluency. Students should practice for accuracy before working on fluency.

127

PROCEDURES

1. **Sound Review**

   Use selected Sound Cards from Units 1–17.

2. **Sounding Out Smoothly**
   - For each word, have students say the underlined part, sound out the word smoothly, then read the whole word. Use the words in sentences, as needed.
   - Have students read all the words in the row, building accuracy first, then fluency.
   - Repeat practice. Mix group and individual turns, independent of your voice.

3. **Accuracy and Fluency Building**
   - For each task, have students say any underlined part, then read each word.
   - Set a pace. Then have students read the whole words in each task and column.
   - Provide repeated practice, building accuracy first, then fluency.

4. **Tricky Words**

   Have students read each row for accuracy, then read the entire grid for fluency.

5. **Multisyllabic Words**

   For each word, have students read each syllable out loud, finger count the syllables, then tell how many syllables are in the word. Have students read the whole word. If needed, use the word in a sentence.

6. **Dictation**
   bird, herd, hard, awful, careful, powerful
   - Say "bird." Have students say the word. Guide students as they finger count and say the sounds. Have students touch or write the sounds, then read the word.

     The first word is **bird.** Say the word. (bird)

     Say and count the sounds in **bird** with me.

     Hold up one finger for each sound. /b/•/ir/•/d/ How many sounds? (three)

     What's the first sound? (/b/) Touch under /b/.

     What's the next sound? (/ir/) Write /ir/ with the letter pattern.

     What's the last sound? (/d/) Touch under /d/.

     Read the word. (bird)

   - Repeat with "herd" and "hard."
   - Continue with the rhyming words: awful, careful, powerful.

Unit 17 Decoding Practice

Name _____

1. **SOUND REVIEW** Use selected Sound Cards from Units 1–17.

2. **SOUNDING OUT SMOOTHLY** Have students say the underlined part, sound out and read each word, then read the row.

| s<u>oi</u>l | shr<u>u</u>b | r<u>i</u>ch | h<u>u</u>ng |

3. **ACCURACY/FLUENCY BUILDING** Have students say any underlined part, then read each word. Next, have students read the column.

A1 Sound Practice	**B1** Rhyming Words	**C1** Buildups	**D1** Tricky Words
fen<u>ce</u>	s<u>ame</u>	<u>po</u>se	lion
lettu<u>ce</u>	n<u>ame</u>	com<u>pose</u>	zebra
	c<u>ame</u>	com<u>pose</u>r	giant
wint<u>er</u>		de<u>compose</u>r	vacant
feed<u>er</u>	**B2** Bossy E		danger
ov<u>er</u>	p<u>i</u>led	cycle	
	gr<u>a</u>zed	recycle	prey
d<u>ea</u>d	h<u>o</u>les	recycled	worm
r<u>ea</u>d	sh<u>a</u>de		neighbors
r<u>ea</u>dy	sh<u>a</u>re	won	scarce
		wonder	
g<u>ar</u>den		wondered	
h<u>ar</u>vest			

4. **TRICKY WORDS** Have students read each row for accuracy, then fluency.

| Ⓐ | walked | walking | watched | wouldn't | warm | 5 |
| Ⓑ | listened | were | pulled | nothing | build | 10 |

5. **MULTISYLLABIC WORDS** Have students read the word by parts, tell how many syllables are in the word, then read the whole word.

Ⓐ	di•gest	digest	de•cay	decay
Ⓑ	com•post	compost	un•der•ground	underground
Ⓒ	pro•tec•ted	protected	to•ma•toes	tomatoes

6. **DICTATION** Say the word. Guide students as they say, finger count, and segment the word. Have students say each sound as they touch or write it.

A1 Shifty Words	**B1** Affixes
b <u>i r</u> d	aw <u>f u l</u>
h er d	c a r e <u>f u l</u>
h <u>a r</u> d	p ow er <u>f u l</u>

PROCEDURES • FLUENCY PASSAGE

1. First Reading
Have students work toward an accuracy goal of 0–2 errors.

2. Second Reading, Timed Reading: Repeated Reading

- Time individual students for 30 or 60 seconds while the other children track with their fingers and whisper read.
- Determine words correct per minute.

3. Partner Reading: Repeated Reading (Checkout Opportunity)

While students do Partner Reading, listen to individuals read the passage.

4. Homework: Repeated Reading

PROCEDURES • ACTIVITY, WORD FLUENCY B

Demonstrate and guide practice, as needed.

1. Activity
Passage Comprehension

Have students read each item, then fill in the bubble and/or blank or write a complete sentence.

Paragraph Comprehension

- Have students read the paragraph.
- Have students read each item, then fill in the bubble and/or blank with the correct answer.

2. Word Fluency (BLMs are located on the CD.)

- Have students read each section three times consecutively.
- To build accuracy, have students read all sets with partners.

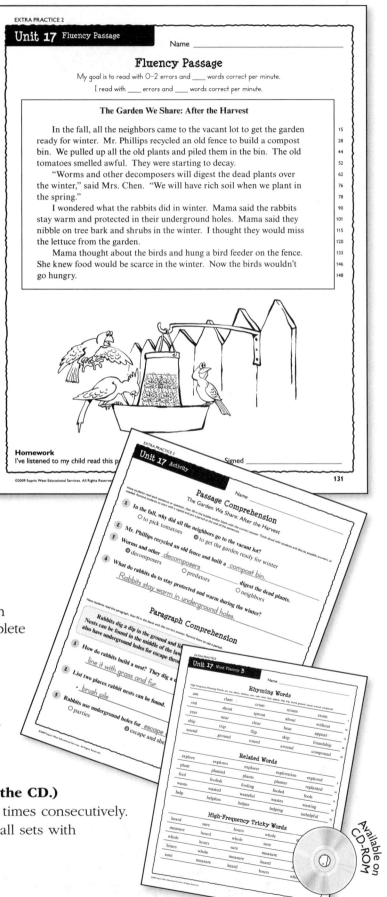

PROCEDURES

1. Sound Review
Use selected Sound Cards from Units 1–17.

2. Sounding Out Smoothly
- For each word, have students say the underlined part, sound out the word smoothly, then read the whole word. Use the words in sentences, as needed.
- Repeat practice. Mix group and individual turns, independent of your voice.

3. Accuracy and Fluency Building
- For each task, have students say any underlined part, then read each word.
- Set a pace. Then have students read the whole words in each task.
- Provide repeated practice, building accuracy first, then fluency.

4. Tricky Words
Have students read each row for accuracy, then read the entire grid for fluency.

5. Multisyllabic Words
For each word, have students read each syllable out loud, finger count the syllables, then tell how many syllables are in the word. Have students read the whole word. If needed, use the word in a sentence.

6. Dictation
send, spend, spent, wide, ride, pride
- Say "send." Have students say the word. Guide students as they finger count and say the sounds. Have students touch or write the sounds, then read the word. Say something like:

  The first word is **send.** Say the word. (send)

  Say and count the sounds in **send** with me.

  Hold up one finger for each sound. /sss/•/ĕĕĕ/•/nnn/•/d/ How many sounds? (four)

  What's the first sound? (/sss/) Touch under /sss/.

  What's the next sound? (/ĕĕĕ/) Write /ĕĕĕ/.

  What's the next sound? (/nnn/) Touch under /nnn/.

  What's the last sound? (/d/) Touch under /d/.

  Read the word. (send)

- Repeat with "spend" and "spent."
- Continue with the rhyming words: wide, ride, pride.

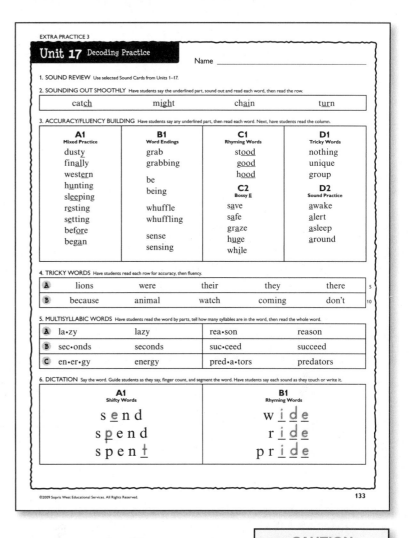

PROCEDURES • FLUENCY PASSAGE

1. First Reading
Have students work toward an accuracy goal of 0–2 errors.

2. Second Reading, Short Passage Practice: Developing Prosody
- Demonstrate and guide how to read a line or two.
- Provide individual turns while others track with their fingers and whisper read.

3. Partner Reading: Repeated Reading (Checkout Opportunity)

4. Homework: Repeated Reading

Have students read the story at home.

PROCEDURES • ACTIVITY, WORD FLUENCY A OR B

1. Activity
Passage Comprehension
- Have students read each sentence or question, then fill in the bubble and/or blank with the correct answer.
- Discuss the multiple-choice options, as needed.

Paragraph Comprehension
- Have students read the paragraph.
- Have students read each sentence or question, then fill in the bubble and/or blank or write a complete sentence.

2. Word Fluency (BLMs are located on the CD.)
You may wish to have students repeat practice with Extra Practice, Word Fluency A or B.